All Abo
Poetry

CW01502066

  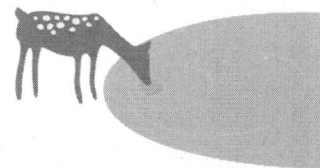

Poems From
The East Midlands

Edited by
Amy Brownlie
& Vivien Linton

This book belongs to

First published in Great Britain in 2010 by

 Young**Writers**

Remus House
Coltsfoot Drive
Peterborough
PE2 9JX
Telephone: 01733 890066
Website: www.youngwriters.co.uk

Foreword

At Young Writers our defining aim is to promote an enjoyment of reading and writing amongst children and young adults. By giving aspiring poets the opportunity to see their work in print, their love of the written word as well as confidence in their own abilities has the chance to blossom.

Our latest competition *Poetry Express* was designed to introduce primary school children to the wonders of creative expression. They were given free reign to write on any theme and in any style, thus encouraging them to use and explore a variety of different poetic forms.

We are proud to present the resulting collection of regional anthologies which are an excellent showcase of young writing talent. With such a diverse range of entries received, the selection process was difficult yet very rewarding.

From comical rhymes to poignant verses, there is plenty to entertain and inspire within these pages. We hope you agree that this collection bursting with imagination is one to treasure.

Contents

The Poems

The Black Mare

The black mare has now gone
No trace of her left but an empty stall.
She'll remain in my heart for evermore
I'll always remember her soft, powdery breath
Tickling my face in clouds of air
The smell of her sweet brown mane.

I remember going to see her, stroking her silky neck,
Watching her pull at the fresh green grass
Swishing her tail with happiness
Those memories are ones to remember.
I imagine she's still there
Alive in my dreams
Galloping onwards through fields
I miss her trotting to greet me.

I have questions to be asked and answered
Where is she now?
What is she doing?
How is she?

She'll live on in me
And I will never ever forget . . .
The black mare.

Annie Johnson (11)
Ashby Willesley Primary School, Ashby De La Zouch

Cricket

I really like to play cricket
I try to strike the wicket
When they hit the round ball
I try to catch them all
When I hit the ball it goes sky-high
Someone catches it so *bye-bye!*

Daniel Evans (10)
Ashby Willesley Primary School, Ashby De La Zouch

The Letter

A letter, a letter
Sometimes I never think better
I wish I met her
Oh, I just love that letter.

A postcard I love
Was sent by my dove
It had a picture of a glove
Oh, I kept that postcard forever.

A text was the best
From my friend in the west
She had found a nest
Oh, I long for that text.

I love to have the best
I need the words' test
I miss staying in touch
Whatever it is, it's not too much
A letter is better
A postcard, not a coastguard
A text, that is next.

Lizzie Townsend (11)
Ashby Willesley Primary School, Ashby De La Zouch

I Am A Trampoline

I am a trampoline
I am bounced on every day
I am big and round in your garden
I am annoying when there is no space to play
I am annoyed when the snow is falling
And people bounce on me
I am happy when the sun is out
And nobody is bouncing on me.

Flora Jarvis (9)
Ashby Willesley Primary School, Ashby De La Zouch

The Tick-Tock Bird

There once was a bird
The tick-tock bird.
It lived up in the wam tree
Just like a tiddly widdly dee
But one day there was a blast
And now Tim is the last
They used to eat Kac Kacs
But Tim only ate Tic-Tacs
They were yellow and blue
And they only wore one shoe
They had black eyes
And they all wore ties
But one day it had to end
It was going round the bend
This all happened because pig ate a tart
Which made him fart
The tick-tock bird is no more
So this is the end of the tour.

Nathan Gibson (11)
Ashby Willesley Primary School, Ashby De La Zouch

The Workmen And The Silver Lining

Every great workman has a silver lining
But every bad workman always blames his tools.
Every dog has his day because it has a great mind
And great minds think alike.
The workman spoilt the broth
Because he was once bitten
Have an apple instead of a feast
Get to the fire even if you are late
The dog might as well have a feast
Instead of a small loaf.

Harriet Bull (11)
Ashby Willesley Primary School, Ashby De La Zouch

Waves

The waves crashing down on the beach
Falling on the sand
The big ones are so loud and noisy
Especially when they land.

Children watching seagulls
Swooping down at the fish
Flying for those children
Would be a wish.

Lots of dudes surfing
All day long
As there's a band on the beach
Singing their song!

People swimming on me
Having lots of fun
But now this poem
Is all over and done!

Louis Adlam (11)
Ashby Willesley Primary School, Ashby De La Zouch

Dream On!

The football came rising high
Fell down near my foot
Kicked it back and the ball swerved away
In the air
The crowd went silent
Until the ball smashed
The back of the net
The ground was roaring
With cheers all around
As I scored to win the World Cup!

James Senior (11)
Ashby Willesley Primary School, Ashby De La Zouch

I Am A Football

I am a football, bouncy and spotty
Every day you kick me
I can't believe you're playing near a window ledge
Oh Heavens! Is that a spiky hedge?

Now I'm a football, flat and squished
Near a river talking to fish
Oh wait, here you come
Please pick me up and take me home.
Wait a second, what's in your hand?
Yes, a pump, now I've been found!

Again, I'm a football being kicked
Please, oh please
Don't play near a window ledge
Because I'll end up in a blooming hedge.

Alex White (9)
Ashby Willesley Primary School, Ashby De La Zouch

The Hamster!

It was as dark as night
With patches of white
Darkness hung in the air
Everyone was asleep
No one awake
No one seemed to care
The hamster opened her black eyes
She crawled out
Furry but wise.

She licked the bowl longingly for food
She looked at me
Sniffing my knee
Sometimes I never see the beauty beneath the fluff.

Katie Smith (11)
Ashby Willesley Primary School, Ashby De La Zouch

I Am A Teddy!

I am a teddy, cute as can be
Shaped as a busy bumblebee
I lie in a cot all day long
I always feel I don't belong
Because Baby hugs all teddies except one
And that one is always me.
It's obvious because you see
I am as big as Baby
Then one day I get thrown out
Because Baby is not about
I go to his friend. She is nice.
OK, I like this
Will I stay?
Because I want to go and play.

Isabella Paduano (7)
Ashby Willesley Primary School, Ashby De La Zouch

I Am A Pair Of Trousers

I am a pair of trousers
You put me on once
But never again
Here you come, I hang up straight
You look in and see me
You choose my fate
You pick me out
You put me on
Then I hear it,
'Mum, these trousers don't fit!'
You take me off
I flop to the ground
Never to be seen again
I'm off to someone thin.

William Statham (9)
Ashby Willesley Primary School, Ashby De La Zouch

Turtle

He's green, he's cuddly
His name begins with T
He's cute and he's cuddly
His name begins with T
It's *turtle*
Turtle
It's *turtle*
Turtle
He bounces all around
He lives in the sea
It's *turtle*
Turtle
It's *Turtle*
Turtle!

Reuben Oakley (11)
Ashby Willesley Primary School, Ashby De La Zouch

Cat And Mouse

It was night
The headlamps were shining bright
At first sight the cat prowled through the night.
Its tail swished from side to side
A mouse was scuttling through the light of the moon
It pounced on the mouse
And took it in the house.

But the house was locked
And the clock went *tick-tock*
The cat woke up next morning
Feeling really quite boring
The mouse was no more
As the cat sat next to the door.

Daniel Edgecombe (11)
Ashby Willesley Primary School, Ashby De La Zouch

Where Are My Pets?

I had a dog called Ginger
In disguise it was a Ninja
Where is it now?

I had a pig called Nagent
In disguise it was an agent
Where is it now?

I had a hamster called Kyeman
In disguise it was a fireman
Where is it now?

I had a lizard called Teesman
In disguise it was a policeman
Where is it now?

Joe Owen (10)
Ashby Willesley Primary School, Ashby De La Zouch

Proverbs Peculiar

New brooms make light work
If every dog has its day
Many hands make light work
And too many cooks sweep clean.
When the cat's away the dogs have their day.
Let sleeping dogs lie and once bitten, dogs lie.
Too many cooks make light work
But only if great minds think alike.
Also every cloud will never hurt me
But I'll be as snug as a bug with a silver lining.
Great minds laugh their heads off
And a bad workman saves nine.
All's well keeps the doctor away.

Emily Torson (11)
Ashby Willesley Primary School, Ashby De La Zouch

Fun In The Snow

I love to play in the snow
It makes my fingers tingle and glow
I love to slide on the ice
I think the snow is very nice.

The December frost is crispy and white
It's a great big blanket of white delight
I love to build lots of snowmen
And then I build a great big snow den.

My friends and I have a snowball fight
But if I don't wear gloves I will get frostbite
I love to go skiing and go on a sledge
Passing the icicles on my window ledge.

Adam Essex (11)
Ashby Willesley Primary School, Ashby De La Zouch

I'm Not Loved

In the shop I sit
Soon you come
You pick me up
'Mummy, Mummy
I want him!'
You take me to the counter.

At home you pull my eye out
And then my ear
'Mummy, Mummy, he's broken.'
'That's not good is it dear?'

Now I'm being sewn up for the second time
Now I'm left, never touched again!

Eleanor Wilde (8)
Ashby Willesley Primary School, Ashby De La Zouch

Nice

The city of Nice
Has lots of palm trees
You could surf the waves
In the gentle breeze.

There's a promenade path
With a stone archway
And a really nice park
Where you can play.

There's a gorgeous hotel
With beautiful pools
And a brilliant spa
That is shiny and cool.

Zoe Weatherley (8)
Ashby Willesley Primary School, Ashby De La Zouch

I Am A Tennis Racquet

I am a racquet, with a ball at my feet
And strings across my face
I tighten my strings and get ready for the match.

Oh look, it's you
You come towards me
Who will you choose? Oh who?
You come towards me, I brace myself
You pick me up, oh how good it feels.

Oh look, we're on our way to the match
Oh, how proud I am
Victory!
Game, set and match!

Thomas Wilson (8)
Ashby Willesley Primary School, Ashby De La Zouch

I Am A Football

I am a football, black and white
I get kicked about
I hope to win, but I hate to doubt.

I am a football, bouncy and round
On a football match they normally bet
'Goal!' they cheer when I'm in the net.

The World Cup is now in my hands
Come on England, forget about all those medal bands
This is the last stand!

Scott Willday (8)
Ashby Willesley Primary School, Ashby De La Zouch

A Random Poem

A bad workman always blames his tools
And every dog has its day
Enough is as good as a feast
So let the dogs lie
Empty vessels have silver linings
A miss is as good as a mile
And all's well that ends well
Let sleeping dogs keep the doctors away
And when the cat's away the dog has its day.

Tabitha Williams (11)
Ashby Willesley Primary School, Ashby De La Zouch

The Babysitter

Babysitters are mardy
No sweets or treats
Can't wait till Mum arrives back
To have some sweets and treats.

They are mean and cruel
Have strict rules, bed early
Babysitters are mean
Do you agree?

Hayley Maria Joesbury (10)
Ashby Willesley Primary School, Ashby De La Zouch

In The Summer

In the summer everyone is happy
Because it is sunny
Everyone is running around
Laughing is the sound
They all go to the beach
One little boy always eats a peach
When it is sunny
Joy is the theme!

Tilly Lewis (11)
Ashby Willesley Primary School, Ashby De La Zouch

The Ball

It was bouncy and blue
I kicked it with my shoe
It was round
Rolling on the ground
I kicked it high
Into the sky.

Stephen Hunt (10)
Ashby Willesley Primary School, Ashby De La Zouch

I Am A Chair

I am a chair, all tatty and old
I rock up and down but do not fall
The door opens, I straighten my spine
In he comes, he walks to me
I rock up and down thinking it's me
He brings a box that's waiting for me
He shoves me in it, I don't know why
I get shredded to pieces, bye-bye.

James Wright (8)
Ashby Willesley Primary School, Ashby De La Zouch

I Am A Lollipop

I am a lollipop
Slimy and round
I am multicoloured
From the top to the ground
I sit on my own
Please get me
It's so cold in here
Will you get me out?

Imogen Grace Banton (8)
Ashby Willesley Primary School, Ashby De La Zouch

I Am A Pencil

I am a pencil, long and sharp
I am lying on a desk waiting for you to use me
You come along and pick me up
And then you start to write on a card
Ow! You press on too hard
Now I am snapped.

Connor Greenwood (7)
Ashby Willesley Primary School, Ashby De La Zouch

I Am A Sea

Blue and big
Really deep
You can swim in me
And have so much fun.

There are lots of animals in me
They are deadly, so vicious to me
I am a blue sea.

Zac Warriner (9)
Ashby Willesley Primary School, Ashby De La Zouch

Proverbs Peculiar

Fire is a good servant but every cloud gathers no moss
Great minds think better late than never
A bad workman always blames his empty vessels
Birds of a feather let sleeping dogs lie

A bad workman flocks together to let sleeping dogs lie
Enough is as good as a mile
When cats are away great minds think alike.

Lauren Brookes (10)
Ashby Willesley Primary School, Ashby De La Zouch

I Am A Cat

I am a cat, pretty and fat
I am a cat, a tabby cat
I am a cat, all black and white
I am a cat, fluffy and spotty
I am a cuddling and snuggling cat
There are my kittens
Where are their mittens?

Remie Smith (8)
Ashby Willesley Primary School, Ashby De La Zouch

Crucifixion

Jesus hanging on the Cross
It was a cheerless day
Overcast in broken black
Cloudy, dim and grey
If only they could set Him free,
'My God, my God, why have You forsaken me?'

Belinda Essex (9)
Ashby Willesley Primary School, Ashby De La Zouch

The Sea

I go out and in all day long
I roar down the beach while people ride me
Then I rest slowly, calmly at night
The moon pulls me back and forth
After that I crash into the sand
With rocks smashing with fresh water sliding off.

Fraser Davies Hearfield (11)
Ashby Willesley Primary School, Ashby De La Zouch

I Am A Teddy Bear

I am a teddy bear, fluffy and fair
My tummy is chubby
My hands in the air
I have ribbons around
My ears that are a lovely bright yellow
And I am a very hands-on fellow.

Lucy Goodvin (8)
Ashby Willesley Primary School, Ashby De La Zouch

I Am A Cat

I am a cat
I am a tabby jabby cat
I jab people because they give me the wrong thing to eat
They give me rice
But I chase after mice.

Robbie Booth (8)
Ashby Willesley Primary School, Ashby De La Zouch

Miss

Miss,
Why are sausages called sausages?
Where do babies come from?
What is the capital of London?
Why do we eat sweetcorn?

Miss,
Why do my dad's sock smell?
How do we die?
Why do fairies live?
How can I fly?

Miss,
How old am I in days?
What is a dictionary?

Children, I've got a question for you
Tell me the square root of 64!

Bethany Field (11)
Barlborough Primary School, Barlborough

Chocolate!

Chocolate, chocolate
Here and there
Chocolate, chocolate
Everywhere.

I like dipping a strawberry in
But never put it in the bin

Chocolate, chocolate
Here and there
Chocolate, chocolate
Everywhere.

Melted, hard, soft and crunchy
No matter what state
I *love* to munchy, munchy!

Chocolate, chocolate
Here and there
Chocolate, chocolate
Everywhere.

There are lots of different truffles, truffles
They make my mouth go *muffle, muffle*.

Chocolate, chocolate
Here and there
Chocolate, chocolate
Everywhere.

Chewy and moist, it can only be Hoist
Hoist is the name of a chocolate shop
It makes me want to shop, shop, shop!

Chocolate, chocolate
Here and there
Chocolate, chocolate
Everywhere!

Savannah Pettinger (11)
Barlborough Primary School, Barlborough

Planets

Mercury is the closest planet to the sun
It has a rocky surface
In the day the temperature can reach over 450 degrees.

Venus is gassy like a dust cloud
Venus is round like a sphere
Venus is small but it can still be seen from Earth.

Earth is blue and green
Earth is like a crystal
Earth is very old and very bold.

Mars is red and very bright
Mars is like a light in the sky
Mars is round and very rocky.

Jupiter is massive
The biggest of the planets
Jupiter has gigantic moons
Jupiter has an enormous storm on it
Which has been raging on for thousands of years.

Saturn is cool, it has 7 rings
Saturn is smooth like a pillow
Saturn looks like it has some wings.

Uranus is deep in space
Uranus is very cold
Uranus can be very bright
If you look through a telescope.

Neptune is blue and very shiny
Neptune is like the sea
Neptune is cold, it has no life
Poor old Neptune, all by itself.

Jack Ezard (11)
Barlborough Primary School, Barlborough

Gordon · The Gingerbread Man!

Gordon the gingerbread man lives on Jury Lane
He likes to play a special game
He'll dance and prance all day long
Singing this song . . .
'Run, run, as fast as you can
You can't catch me, I'm the gingerbread man!'

He has a button nose and little round toes
Pale blue eyes and a blood-red mouth
He'll never smile down towards south
Always north, smiley and cheeky
Drinking from the milk pipe when it gets leaky!

I love having Gordon around to my house
He's always as quiet as a mouse
He's special and pure and the one I adore!

Phoebe Allatt (11)
Barlborough Primary School, Barlborough

I Give My All!

When he exits the tunnel and enters the pitch, he's ace
Rocketing down the left wing providing crosses for Tevez and Barry
The manager hates him, he doesn't care
He slides on the floor and gets booked for dissent
He loves the crowd and the crowd loves him
He hates Man United

He's had a fair share of goals this season
With mind-blowing goals against United, Chelsea and Arsenal too
He bullets down the left wing leaving defenders stood stump still
When he shoots and scores
Goalkeepers go red in the face with embarrassment
He has number 39 written on his shirt
His name is Bellamy and he gives his all.

Alex Watson (11)
Barlborough Primary School, Barlborough

Summer

Summer sun means summer fun
Suntan - where's the ice cream van?
Water fights on the back
Waiting for the sprinkler to crack!

Summer afternoon,
Please tell Liam to stop being a loon
Water guns go to rest
This is where your head gets a test!

Summer night, looking at a bright light
Chiminea spits out ash
I've just heard a big *crash!*
I think it might be time to end the day
Ready for another summery play!

Amy Jackson (10)
Barlborough Primary School, Barlborough

Goalkeeping

As you walk onto the lush, green pitch
With your head in a turmoil ditch
When the coach brings you over after he overslept
He tells you the tactics then you walk into the net
The match has started, and a striker is coming
You give them the glare but they really don't care
It's too late, he is at the edge of the box
He shoots, it's *going in*, but who is there?
The keeper, of course,
As the striker falls down with a heart full of shame
Proudly, the keeper gets up with a heart full of fame
Finally the match is over, they settle with a draw
But I don't really care, I made the best save of them all . . .

Benjamin Lodge (11)
Barlborough Primary School, Barlborough

Summer Fun

The sky peers through the candyfloss clouds
As the sun beats down on the land
Families paddle in the sea
Play on the scorching sand
Underwater creatures pop up to say hello
Then splash back down below
Coral waters, tropical fish, create an aqua odyssey
As they swim around in circles and blush with modesty.

When you go on picnics, pollen goes up your nose
When you go on picnics, the grass tickles your toes
The best thing about picnics, you have a chocolate cake
The best thing about picnics, you see ducks by the lake.

Gabriella Everett (11)
Barlborough Primary School, Barlborough

Seasons Of The Year

Cold ice may not make people feel nice
Winter is cold
Winter is freezing
People think it is not very pleasing.

The sun is hot, people like it a lot
The sun is blistering
Even when you use your Listerine.

The leaves in autumn are very crispy
But the mist around my ankles is very misty

The flowers in spring may open up
Then you will find a buttercup.

Finley Messenger (11)
Barlborough Primary School, Barlborough

Zebra Stripes!

Zebra stripes, black, white
Useful for camouflage for predators in sight
Each stripe is truly unique
But never dull, not the same as an American bull!
Zebras flash in the bright sunrise
As people come to give their praise.

Hunters hunt for the bright stripes
People will pay to put them on display
The stripes are used for coats
Which is a fashion accessory
Even though it is not necessary.

Lewis Kitcheman (11)
Barlborough Primary School, Barlborough

Rabbits!

Rabbits, rabbits everywhere
Rabbits, rabbits, descendants of hares
I've got one called Snowflake
I've got one called Branston
I'm sure he'd like to try pickle
Rabbits, rabbits, some big, some small
Rabbits, rabbits, I love them all
They're rabbits, they rabbits
They're rabbits.

Mitchell Kitcheman (11)
Barlborough Primary School, Barlborough

Buddy Thinks

Buddy thinks he's David Beckham
Buddy thinks he can fly
Buddy thinks he can walk on water
He thinks it's impossible to die
He's one in a million
He's worth a billion
Definitely sky-high!

Evangeline Cull (11)
Barlborough Primary School, Barlborough

Funky Bear

Funky bear yawning, Funky bear sad
Funky bear sleeping, Funky bear glad
Funky bear hungry, Funky bear frowning
Funky bear eating, Funky bear *smiling!*

Gregory Cox (11)
Barlborough Primary School, Barlborough

What Is Fear?

Fear tastes like bones, for a dangerous dog's dinner.
Fear is the colour of darkness creeping along
Through the streets like a black cat.
Fear is a dark forest, where spiders and wood elves lurk
Fear smells of rotting flesh on a battlefield
Fear feels like darkness moving slowly onto the sky
Fear sounds like war cries being chanted
From one army to the other like a tennis ball.

William Howells (10)
Bassingham Primary School, Bassingham

The New Girl

The terrified new girl stood all alone
Just wishing to go home
Feeling eyes upon her gaze
Looking as if she's in a daze.

The bell goes
Everybody rushes in like a hurricane
Everybody thinks she's going to be a pain

She sits on the carpet feeling lonely and small
She bunches up in a scared ball
The teacher's sharp voice calls out her name
But she's just sitting there like it's a game

So now if anyone knew
What she has to go through
They'd make her have a better day
And make sure she's OK.

Ellie Hackett (11)
Bassingham Primary School, Bassingham

What Is Happiness?

Happiness smells of all the different animals
That all seem like they are holding happiness forever.
Happiness feels warm and safe from the sun
Which is glistening down on everything.
Happiness is pink like the beautiful, velvet blossom.
Happiness looks like birds singing in the warm, swaying breeze.
Happiness tastes like all the hard work we have done this summer.
Happiness sounds like children laughing on a hot summer's day.

Amber Owens (10)
Bassingham Primary School, Bassingham

On My Way To School

Past the chimpanzee
Walking over the barking tree
Under the massive root
Stumbling over the human boot!

Away on the magic carpet
Tripping over the fishing net
Sailing on the tiny boat
Where Postman Pat is buying a new coat.

Walking through the gate
Oh no, I'm going to be late
My teacher's going to be mad
So mad she's phoning my dad!

Charlotte Ripley (11)
Bassingham Primary School, Bassingham

In The Sky

There's a world, a world in the sky
No one knows, no one but I
It's on a cloud, fluffy and light
It's pink, blue or even white.

Now and then a feather falls down
Onto the Earth that's square or round
In the clouds the highest of all
There's a purple castle with turrets
That go high, high, higher than the clouds
High, high, higher than the planets
When at the top you feel dizzy and sick
Because you sway in a thick, thick mist.

Molly Ellen Fosh (10)
Bassingham Primary School, Bassingham

What Is Fun?

Fun feels like running around free in a fresh meadow
Fun is yellow, shining in the glowing sun, spreading around the world
Fun smells like fresh air covering the world like a blanket keeping the
fresh air in
Fun sounds like girls and boys screaming and shouting with laughter
Fun tastes like your first step into a lake, cold on your feet
Fun looks like happy faces and smiles on children's faces.

Maisy Mitchell (10)
Bassingham Primary School, Bassingham

What Is Surprise?

Surprise is like the first smile of a baby when he has been born
Surprise tastes like a firework going off in your mouth
Surprise sounds like happy children playing in the park
Surprise feels like a lion cub being born
Surprise is black and white like a whale splashing about in a blue
lagoon
Surprise smells like the last star burning out.

Elliot Owen Doody (10)
Bassingham Primary School, Bassingham

What Is Fear?

Fear tastes like a big, prickly spider crawling down your throat
Fear is black, like a dark cave with ghosts
Fear feels like you are falling out of the sky with no parachute
Fear sounds like big footsteps climbing up the steps
Fear looks like you're trapped in a dungeon
Fear smells like smoke coming out of the house and you're in it.

Callum Wiseman (10)
Bassingham Primary School, Bassingham

What Is Silence?

Silence is like a black nothingness creeping over the world
Silence smells like fresh air, you and I breathe in
Silence tastes like cold, bitter air, swirling all around me
Silence is golden, looping mounds of corn
Silence feels comforting, glad to be alone
Silence sounds like a plain, blank sheet of paper.

Elizabeth Airdrie (10)
Bassingham Primary School, Bassingham

What Is Love?

Love feels like a warm and cuddly blanket
Love tastes like a yummy, juicy apple
Love looks like a pond gleaming in the sun
Love sounds like the birds tweeting in the trees
Love smells like perfume of a rose
Love is as white as a fluffy sheep.

Robert Braithwaite (10)
Bassingham Primary School, Bassingham

What Is Surprise?

Surprise feels like an electric shock in the body
Surprise sounds like a million threats
Surprise smells of scariness or a good jubilant party
Surprise tastes of fun and horror mixed together
Surprise looks like jolly and joy on a picture frame
Surprise is red, full of hatred!

Stefan Taylor (10)
Bassingham Primary School, Bassingham

What Is Fun?

Fun is rainbow-coloured, like a family gathering
Fun feels like a never-ending journey
Fun sounds like the sun giggling with me
Fun looks like a garden with adorable flowers
Fun smells like laughter and joy
Fun tastes like a downpour of happiness.

Annabelle Traves (10)
Bassingham Primary School, Bassingham

What Is Happiness?

Happiness is gold like a ray of happy sunshine
Happiness looks like the first kiss under a shower of moonlight
Happiness tastes like strawberry lipgloss on her sweet lips
Happiness sounds like a bird singing its sweet song
Happiness smells of sweet chocolate
Happiness feels like a warm glow inside your heart.

Megan Cerys Thompson (10)
Bassingham Primary School, Bassingham

What Is Fun?

Fun looks like children playing in a summer breeze
Fun tastes like chips, as friends eat and laugh with each other
Fun sounds like a child's laughter after someone tells a joke
Fun smells like fruit and crisps at a birthday party
Fun feels like mayhem, as children run wild around a house
Fun is blue like age flags at a birthday party.

Alexander Lee (9)
Bassingham Primary School, Bassingham

What Is Fear?

Fear is red, screaming, hatred and pain, the anger of a lost one
Fear is black, a cage in the corner, a dark, deserted corner
Fear is green, an alien in the kitchen, the strong smell of sweets
Fear is red, the taste of blood, cold blood fit for a vampire
Fear is blue, a ship sinking into the dark blue water
Fear is grey, like the breeze of a thunderstorm.

Samuel Carlisle (9)
Bassingham Primary School, Bassingham

What Is Courage?

Courage is green like a four leaf clover pinned to your heart
Courage smells like fear holding you back
Courage tastes like lemons, sour but sweet
Courage looks so jolly and cheerful
Courage feels like a lion's mane brushing against your skin
Courage sounds like a mouse squeak, fear is upon you!

Harriet Berrington-Hughes (10)
Bassingham Primary School, Bassingham

What Is Love?

Love is the colour of brown like a teddy bear.
Love feels like red-hot sun.
Love tastes like a juicy, cooked steak.
Love looks like red silk on a wedding dress
Love sounds like birds singing in a tree.
Love smells like cooked food.

Hayden Joseph Laughton (9)
Bassingham Primary School, Bassingham

What Is Fun?

Fun sounds like laughs flowing in the breeze.
Fun tastes like happiness flowing around.
Fun looks like a rainbow blowing through the wind.
Fun is red like a cherry river flowing along.
Fun smells of flowers on a summer day.
Fun feels like warm happiness in your heart.

Eloise Faulkner (9)
Bassingham Primary School, Bassingham

What Is Happiness?

Happiness tastes like a bowl of fun on a hot summer's day
Happiness sounds like laughter floating all around
Happiness smells like cherries, luxurious and ripe
Happiness is red with a little bit of love
Happiness looks like romance with a topping of friendship.

Lydia Larocque (10)
Bassingham Primary School, Bassingham

My Boat

My boat is a topper
It is 11ft long with two 5 metre sails
Its hull is snow-white and the deck is bright red
It has got a jet-black winch and a nice red 'rooster sailing' toe strap.

My boat goes like a rocket when sailing the seven seas
It leaves a large cloud of spray gleaming in her stern
And great waves surfing along behind to indicate where I have gone.

My boat runs through the water like a pack of wolves
Searching for enemies to eat like mice
But when the wind makes a runner and there is no one left to play
My boat is a different soul, so peaceful and calm.

Alexander Cook (10)
Blakesley CE Primary School, Blakesley

My Imaginary Friend

My imaginary friend
Has a body like mine
A head of a dragon and feel like a horse's
Burnishing hooves.

My imaginary friend
Turns inconspicuous whenever he chooses
Spooking people when he likes
Watch out for my friend.

My imaginary friend
Likes to devour food
His favourite food is air
He likes to quaff water, fresh water.

My imaginary friend
Is exhilaratingly and happily running around
In my head in a large open space
He'll never get upset.

My imaginary friend
Vaults out at intruders
But to me he's a great friend, very soft
I love my imaginary friend!

Billie Edwards (10)
Blakesley CE Primary School, Blakesley

A Tiger

A slick strider
A stylish sprinter
A striped skinner
With piercing eyes.

A muscle merchant
A boisterous bounder
A fighting figure
With colossal canines.

A rainforest ruler
A moonlight minder
A proud pouncer
With tin-opening claws.

An intelligent instructor
An ancient agoniser
An aggressive assassin
With a snarling growl!

Laura Simpson (11)
Blakesley CE Primary School, Blakesley

The Race

It's the end of qualifying
I'm in pole
I walk over to my Ferrari
Made with passion and soul.

I'm in the driving seat
Looking at the lights
They go red, yellow then green
We're off! What a scene!

Round the first corner
Hit a rubber turd
I spin off
That cost me third.

On the home straight
I'm in first place
Oh my goodness
I've won the race!

George Noble (11)
Blakesley CE Primary School, Blakesley

Fire-Breather

Don't go into the gloomy passage
Don't choke in the room . . . or it will get you
When you reach the dark cave, remember what it does!
Remember the smoke can kill you
The fire-breather is dangerous. *Beware!*
It's a jewel keeper, leave it alone or it will get you!
Its fiery breath, its silky wings
It can fly as high as the sun. So *beware!*
Its back is spiky and as sharp as axes
It will cut you!
It's as red as blood and its eyes are blue
Its stomach is covered with beautiful gems
Its skin is so soft but deadly with fear
So *beware!*
Next time you see a fire-breather
Run and never come back!
So beware!

Elena Zajko (10)
Blakesley CE Primary School, Blakesley

I Wish I Could Fly!

I wish I could fly
Imagine what I could do!

I could spread out my wings
And soar like an eagle.

I could fly to France
And come back in time for lunch!

I could fly to the clouds
And wave to the planes below.

I could fly to school
I would never be late.

I could fly around the world in just one day
And stop off in every country.

I wish I could fly
Imagine what I could do!

Isabella Lyon (11)
Blakesley CE Primary School, Blakesley

Chelsea FC

Such power they have
Such talent as well
The shots almost burst the net!

The Blues is their nickname
They play in full blue
Their mascot is called Stamford
He is blue too.

My favourite players are Anelka
And Florent Malouda too
A left wing and striker
But the other players are brilliant too.

There's only one question left . . .
Who is this brilliant team?
Well, it's got to be *Chelsea!*

Robert Chambers (10)
Blakesley CE Primary School, Blakesley

My Cat

My cat is very adorable
She is called Minty
Minty loves rolling in cat mint
Then chasing all the butterflies.

She is the prettiest and cutest cat
In the whole wide world
Her body is very silky
And it is black and white.

Minty has the greenest emerald eyes
That glisten in the sun
At night she comes on my bed
And goes to sleep!

Samantha Adams (10)
Blakesley CE Primary School, Blakesley

Grandparents

Grandparents are cool, wearing tiny sphere-shaped glasses.
They're always leaving bags of sweets round the house,
Merrily gobbling them as they go
From the minute they arrive, they're always giving you sloppy kisses
And bone-crushing hugs.
They're only showing you love and affection
But it does get disturbing
Mum and Dad may say, 'Just please be quiet!'
Always saying things twice
But this time at full volume
Enough to deafen a sharp-eared teacher
Grandparents can sometimes look like clothes that haven't been
ironed
Grandparents are like small piggy banks with holes in
Overall, I think grandparents are amazing!

Cobi Welsh (11)
Blakesley CE Primary School, Blakesley

My Pony

My pony is very, very fluffy
His fur is as soft as silk
And it gleams in the sun.

My pony is as good as gold
He always does what he is told
And he never does anything naughty.

My pony is exceedingly tall
He is 14.2 hands high
And is hard to mount from the ground.

My pony is rather friendly
He follows me everywhere
And he is so cute!

Georgia Summers (11)
Blakesley CE Primary School, Blakesley

My Dog

My dog is called Tod
He is a Cocker Spaniel
His nose is black like jewels
He is cute, cuddly and adorable
His ears are black and floppy
I think he is ridiculously fluffy
He adores having long walks
Especially with his friend Poppy
He is hyper and can be lazy too
He walks along with big, padding feet
Like a bear
As you approach the door
He will bark his head off
And run up and down skidding on the carpet
I love him very much!

Emily Patricia Colts-Tegg (10)
Blakesley CE Primary School, Blakesley

Spring Things

Spring has things like:
Clouds as soft as cotton candy
Chicks as yellow as a sunflower
Grass as green as lettuce
Spring has things like:
Lambs springing around the field
The sun beating down on the animals' coats
New flowers shooting up like rabbits hopping.
Spring has things like:
A deer trying to get used to its wobbly legs
Animals silky, glossy, gleaming in the sun
Rainbows appearing in the blue sky.

Linzi Bandtock (10)
Blakesley CE Primary School, Blakesley

My Teddy

My teddy is soft and fluffy
He wears a yellow T-shirt
With two black paw prints on the front
And a red rocket
He is ginger in colour
With a black nose and shiny eyes
He has a small tail, small arms
But big legs
He carries a yellow and brown pot
With yummy honey dripping out
His name is Ted
He is the best!

George Jackson (10)
Blakesley CE Primary School, Blakesley

Pure Love

Pure energy flowing through your heart
As white as a fresh snowflake
Feels as soft as silk
Cosy as a hot cup of cocoa on a cold winter's day.

Hand-made by angels up above
As tasty as a sweet shop
Smells like a million roses delicately hand-picked
It has an amazing aftertaste.

A delicacy not to be broken
Sounds like the beautiful cry of a baby
A perfect paradise
The reason of living.

Joseph Perkin (11)
Cedar Road Primary School, Northampton

Anger's A Curse

Anger is a feeling that never decays
It's like a raging bull
Never hitting the red cloth
Anger's a curse.

Anger is the colour of fire
Flaring up and never going out
It's also a slab of ice so cold to the touch
Making life so cold that ice never melts
Anger's a curse.

Anger tastes like spicy hot sauce
Boiling the tongue and making a burn
It's like a dog chasing its tail
But it will never succeed
Anger's a curse.

And anger will leave when he apologises
And the curse will forever be lost
But still, anger's a curse.

Luke Yuill (11)
Cedar Road Primary School, Northampton

Love!

Love tastes like candyfloss melting away in your mouth
Red is like a million roses for loved ones
Love is like birds tweeting away to a love song
Love, love and love
Love smells like roses falling on you gently
Love feels like a cosy warm afternoon with each other
Love, love and love
Love is the sound of water swaying gently down the stream
Love is lovely.

Aniqa Ali (10)
Cedar Road Primary School, Northampton

Revenge Is Sweet

Revenge is as sweet as the 1p sweet shop
On the corner of the street
With an old wicked woman working there.

Revenge is grey, all the colours mixed together
Waiting to pop and surprise everyone.

Revenge is a grandfather clock
Ticking in your head over and over again
For as long as it takes to make the other person
You seek revenge on as mad as you.

Revenge is like someone has shaken you up
Like a fizzy drink waiting to pop and burst open.

Tom Rowlatt (10)
Cedar Road Primary School, Northampton

Anger

Anger is the Devil lying deep beneath the ground
It always has something, a deafening sound

Anger melts, then hardens again
No, it will never hide the pain

Anger, you will have to accept
Sometimes you will never forget

Anger is red-hot, burning in your soul
Anger is hot, as hot as black coal

Oh anger, who made this terrible thing?
Whoever did, put their arm in a sling.

Lauren Dunkley (11)
Cedar Road Primary School, Northampton

Anger, Anger!

Anger is the colour of terrible tomatoes
Vomiting out of your mouth.

Anger is the sound of thunder
That you can hear from down under.

Anger feels like your street burning
Full of streaming smoke.

Anger is the taste of sour sweets
Swelling your tongue.

Anger is the smell of fiery flames
Spitting out from a vicious volcano.

Adil Rahman Abdullah (11)
Cedar Road Primary School, Northampton

Just Like My Fears . . .

Blue is the teardrops running down my face
The frozen lake waiting to be cracked, just like my fears
Gentle tapping of the drum, running through my mind just like my fears
Pea pods bursting out, just like my fears.

Me lying here smells like a block of cheese
Waiting for the hungry mouse, just like my fears
Loud booming from next door's club, making my fears go wild
The rough floorboards poking at me, as irritating as my fears.

Some day a person will have fears, just like my fears.

Georgia White (10)
Cedar Road Primary School, Northampton

Lovely Love

Love, love and love
I think love is the colour of red
Because red is the colour of your heart
To me love feels like a sweet shop
All sugary and sweet
Love is like laying on a bed with petals dropping on you
Love sounds like two little birds singing a love song
Love smells like candyfloss, candyfloss is so sugary and thick
Love, love and love!

Sophie Bennett (10)
Cedar Road Primary School, Northampton

Anger

Anger tastes like Haribo Tangfastics
Dancing and prancing around your tongue
Anger smells like old rotting flesh
Getting worse and worse by the day.

Anger is the colour of red blood
Dripping from a bloodthirsty wolf
Anger sounds like shouts and screams
Coming from the burning pits of Hell.

Ben Tombs (11)
Cedar Road Primary School, Northampton

Love

Love is fluffy pink with Cupid shooting his arrows in random directions
Love smells like a sweet shop with candyfloss and sugar
Love is a bird calling for its lover
Love smells of happiness and liberty for all of eternity.

Henry Kennedy (11)
Cedar Road Primary School, Northampton

Revenge Is Sweet

Cold, sad, scared
Planning to overturn
Powerful, pumping adrenaline
Waiting for the call
Shout, scream, horror
The king's men shout
Run, slam, victory
The rightful king is crowned.

Oliver Geary (11)
Cedar Road Primary School, Northampton

Revenge

Revenge is the colour of dripping, rotten tomatoes
Revenge tastes like sour sherbet popping and sizzling
Revenge sounds like a mischievous lion's thunderous roar
Revenge feels like an uncontrolled animal raging through your body
Revenge is the darkness inside us
Revenge is the knight's fear
Revenge is the victor's happiest feelings
Revenge is what I feel.

Jamie Tarr (10)
Cedar Road Primary School, Northampton

Love!

The colour is a pinkish red flowing as a waterfall of love
Love is like pink, fluffy roses
It tastes like a thousand candyflosses, fizzing on your tongue
Love is as tough as anything that you can't overcome
What do you think it is?

Charlotte Lavender (10)
Cedar Road Primary School, Northampton

Revenge Is Easy

Revenge is the ear-piercing sound of a scream
Maybe the scream of the victim of your revenge.
Revenge is the roughness of a pine cone.
Revenge is as easy as killing an ant.
But is as sour as a lemon.
Revenge is the smell of rotting bodies
Revenge is the savage, blood-curdling red
Revenge is the sleepless and unending night.

James Pierce (11)
Cedar Road Primary School, Northampton

Love

Love is red as a rose
It tastes like sweet, sugary candyfloss
It sounds like a butterfly's wings
It feels like fluffy toys
It smells like strawberry candles.

Chloe Morris (10)
Cedar Road Primary School, Northampton

Revenge, Revenge!

Revenge, revenge is easy-peasy as it can be
Revenge is sour and bitter like lychees
Revenge feels nervous and angry like an elephant
Revenge is bloodstained clothes
Revenge sounds like people going to their death.

Thomas Giles (11)
Cedar Road Primary School, Northampton

Revenge

Revenge is a nuke destroying the world
Revenge is the taste of a blood cocktail
Revenge is a field of dead people laying on the floor
Revenge is a slippy, over-heated alien
Revenge is a fiery jungle.

Ally O'Dell (11)
Cedar Road Primary School, Northampton

Anger

Anger is the colour of deep, dark black
Anger tastes sour, strong and gross
Anger sounds like thunder roaring all over the Earth
Anger feels mad, crazy, although lost
Anger smells like a fire mixed with a deadly poison.

Amie Williams (10)
Cedar Road Primary School, Northampton

Revenge!

Revenge tastes like fire burning the roof off your mouth
Revenge sounds like a proud, tall-standing lion
Revenge feels like a boiling kettle melting through your hand
Revenge smells like blazing petrol.

Connor Doble (11)
Cedar Road Primary School, Northampton

Do Your Homework

Do your homework
Or there'll be trouble
Maybe you'll get trapped
Inside a bubble
Or you'll meet your evil double.

Do your homework
Don't be a detentioner
Sitting in class
For hours and hours
By the time you get out
You'll be a pensioner.

Do your homework
You'll be a good kid
Not in detention fiddling with lids
Free to enjoy the wind
Against the classroom
You won't be pinned.

Tasnim Begum (11)
Earl Spencer Primary School, Northampton

A Best Friend

A best friend's for secrets, for giggles and fun
A friend's for hanging out with, indoors or in the sun
A best friend's the best when you're feeling bad
Not to have a best friend is sadder than sad.

Christa Fisher (8)
Earl Spencer Primary School, Northampton

Rebecca Mathers Poem

Her last name is Mathers
She really likes Quavers
Her dog is called Sam
And he really likes jam
She also has a kitten called Tinkerbell
Who plays with her bell
Her brother is Jordan
They both have a grandad called Gordon
She has a friend called Keeley
Who owns a parrot called Heeley
Her cousin is called Ella
Who has a friend called Bella.

Rebecca Mathers (9)
Earl Spencer Primary School, Northampton

Now I've Lost You

Why, oh why did you leave us?
Why leave your family alone?
You will always be missed
You will never be forgotten
But why leave?
And why go?
Why didn't you say goodbye?
Why do you make us cry sometimes?
Why did you want to go or leave?
Where are you now Ben?
Where have you gone?

Joe Lyons (10)
Earl Spencer Primary School, Northampton

Birds Can Fly In Wind

The wind gracefully blew through the valleys
To reach Nelly Bay
Nelly Bay was empty. so wind blew away.

The bird flew gently on its way to sea
The fishermen spotted him
But he safely flew away.

If the wind had blown north
And the bird flew that way
he may have been caught
By fishermen on Nelly Bay.

Lauren Hibberd (10)
Earl Spencer Primary School, Northampton

Silence

It reminds me of when something is uncomfortable.
It reminds me of the cinema, before the film starts
And it says to turn off your phone.
It tastes of nothing, my mouth as wet as water
Because I'm gulping to try and bring back noise.
It makes me feel lonely because I've got nobody to talk to
And everything around goes silent.
It looks like a blank face, just staring at you
Its eyes screaming, shouting for help.
It sounds like the slight sound, but barely noticeable
It slowly stops . . . silence.
Sad, nobody to share my feelings with, I can't say I'm sad
Or I'm lonely, because nobody is there to tell.
A grey wall, just wishing for people to paint it
It wants to be a colourful wall
There's the tin, its last blob, dripping and dying the carpet.

Ella Smith (11)
Furness Vale Primary School, High Peak

Curiosity

Curiosity tastes like space candy exploding on your tongue
Because you are finding something new every minute.
Curiosity is black because you can't see what's coming.
Curiosity smells like freshly poured lemonade
But you still don't know if it will taste nice or not.
Curiosity is like a great big boulder, you don't know where it will
bounce first.
Curiosity sounds like a plane crashing
You don't know if everyone inside the plane will be OK.
Curiosity makes me feel like I am a clock ticking
Because I don't know when I will get to the bottom of the problem.
Curiosity feels like a cobbled road, you don't know when the bumps
will end.
Curiosity reminds me of the times when I had to go inside
Because a gigantic thunderstorm hit.

Shannon Bennett (11)
Furness Vale Primary School, High Peak

Courage

A shout of 1,000 men's battlecries in war as they charge the enemy.
It feels great but scary, because I might die in combat
And prepared for battle with butterflies in my tummy.
Tastes like a hot, raw chilli melting in my mouth.
It reminds me of my two uncles in World War II
When they died for their country.
I hear the men crying in pain and the gunshots and tank rounds
firing.
I smell the burning flesh as the flame-thrower burns my comrade's
face.
The colour of blood splattered on the wall and boots of my men.

Harrison Thorpe (11)
Furness Vale Primary School, High Peak

Love!

Glittery pink and orange too, yellow like amber shining in the sun.
The beautiful smell of roses, sweets and fantastic chocolate.
The beautiful sight of love hearts and flowers that look like diamonds in the moonlight.
It reminds me of holidays in the sun and on the beaches.
Lovely birds in summer and spring that sound like flutes in the summer breeze.
I feel happy and cared for in every single way.
It makes me feel happy and sweet inside
And it tastes like yummy chocolate cake on an empty table.

Grace Collier (11)
Furness Vale Primary School, High Peak

Sadness

It feels like when you get sent to your bedroom when your mum and dad shout at you.
It sounds like when I shout really loud and cry when I hurt myself.
It looks like when I get lost somewhere and I can't find my parents.
It reminds me of when my dad is in hospital and has to stay overnight.
It tastes like cheese rotting away on my plate.
It smells like the salty sea with waves crashing on the rocks.
It makes me feel like a pond with no fish.
The colour is a big bonfire with burning flames on the top.

Sam Huddlestone (11)
Furness Vale Primary School, High Peak

Delight

It reminds me of juicy strawberries and icing sugar.
Sounds like birds cheeping happily in the trees.
Makes me feel as if I want to throw a massive party.
The colour is as blue as the night sky which makes me want to dream.
To me it smells like freshly cut grass quite nearby.
It looks like a giant buffet with lots of sweet things - delicious.
It tastes like home-made chocolate cake which is melting in your mouth.
It feels like soft velvet, so silky.

Laura Jodrell (11)
Furness Vale Primary School, High Peak

Fear

Fear tastes like the tears on my face when I watch a horror movie.
Fear reminds me of the first time I went on the scary maze game
And I didn't know it was scary.
Fear looks like the Exorcist and IT in a room
I shout for help as they advance towards me, argh!
It sounds like the horrible scream on my dad's phone
That was so horrible it made by 8 year old brother cry.
It feels like a torture device
That slowly but surely crushes my head like a balloon popping, bang!

Kevin O'Neill (10)
Furness Vale Primary School, High Peak

Fun

I like fun because it's full of wonderful things:
Like children running around with smiles on their faces, playing
games.
Candyfloss from a funfair and chocolate cake in the shop.
My friends and I playing in grassy, green gardens with colours
covering us.
People laughing and children eating warm, melt-in-the-middle
chocolate cake pudding.
Soft, fluffy blankets, all colours of the rainbow
It just makes me feel like I'm loved and cared for.

Aleah Wood (10)
Furness Vale Primary School, High Peak

Anger

Anger looks like a troll walking down the street
Smashing everything in its way.
It makes me feel like going round shooting everyone with a mini gun.
It sounds like the Hulk screaming and shouting.
It reminds me of my brother stamping down the hallway.
Anger tastes like a horrible, out of date yoghurt.
The colour of anger is red mixed with dark green.
Anger smells of flesh rotting away in a cellar.
It feels rough and hard, like a big boulder.

James Potts (11)
Furness Vale Primary School, High Peak

Surprise

The shouting of your friends when you arrive home
And there is a huge party waiting.
When I first met my best friend on the first day of school.
The extravagant flavours of Thai food when you first taste it.
Surprise makes me feel ecstatic and full of life.
It looks like a huge party with all my friends and family.
I think surprise is bright yellow.
Surprise smells like hot burgers coated in brown sauce.
It feels like the soft fur of a cat rubbing against your leg.

Vanessa Rowlands (11)
Furness Vale Primary School, High Peak

Pain

It makes me feel sad, hurt, unhappy.
It looks like darkness, blood everywhere.
It smells like your own blood and human flesh.
I think the colour of pain is red for blood and black for darkness.
It tastes like gone-off food.
It reminds me of an injury that I had.
I think the sound of pain is people screaming for help.
It feels like running blood and a dead animal.

Jonathon Huddlestone (11)
Furness Vale Primary School, High Peak

The Pier

Mast poles collide on a burning sky
Clouds silhouetted on a smouldering canvas
Sun beats down its final rays
A winking eye, a thousand rubies
A water-colour spectacle
An unknown wonder.
Silent, still, Mother Nature embraces her animals
A view of the world from a place faraway
Grains of golden sand
Fine as sticky, sweet sugar
Not a care in the world
Not a breath of anger or sorrow
No emotion, no fear
Just the pier.

Alice Walker (11)
Hasland Junior School, Chesterfield

Fun And Games

Are you bored with nothing to do?
Pick up a bat and a ball too
Maybe swing on a swing
Or fly through the sky
Climb a tree that's really high.

You can do all these things in just one day
Sing, jump and happily play
You can spin around and get dizzy as can be
Buy a kite for you and me.

Might you swim in a pool, length after length
Kids yell, *'Weeee!'* as they slide down the slide
Then skip home happily just for tea
That's a fun day we've had, just you and me.

Lauren Smith (11)
Hasland Junior School, Chesterfield

Animals Poem

Tigers, boars, pigs and cats
Whales, fish, dogs and bats

Cows, squirrels, dogs and dolphins
Jaguars, lions, rabbits and falcons

Eagles, spiders, penguins and headlice
Zebras, horses, goats and mice

Worms, snails, sheep and bears
Sparrows, lizards, squid and hares

Animals
Which are your favourite?

Bethany Stapleton (11)
Hasland Junior School, Chesterfield

Friends

At school I have lots of friends
When a new kid arrives, it depends,
'Hey,' said Brad Dunnely
Emma laughed funnily
And now they are best friends.

At a club, Layla just bends
My favourite animals are hens
She comes to my house
And plays with my mouse
When she goes, the fun never ends.

Chloe Plevey (11)
Hasland Junior School, Chesterfield

Seaside Dream

The sea, calm and still
Birds chirping so sweetly
Boats gently swaying side to side, so tranquil
The sand, soft and silky
The sky as blue as cornflowers
The sun beaming
Oh I really love the seaside!

Lauren Mee (11)
Hasland Junior School, Chesterfield

The Summer Box
(Inspired by 'Magic Box' by Kit Wright)

I will put in my box . . .
The ice cream in a cone
The horrible grey smoke from the barbecue
Sparkling lemonade ready to drink.

I will put in my box . . .
Licking strawberries with cream
Babies screaming in the park
People sitting in the sun too long.

I will put in my box . . .
Bright yellow bees on your flowers
A drop of white ice cream on your arm
Lovely green grass under your feet.

I will put in my box . . .
Brown Lemonade and see-through Coke
Green sun and yellow trees
Blue leaves and green blueberries.

My box is fashioned with Magnum golds
Shiny shell corners
The lid made of dead rainbow fish
Its hinges are stars.

I shall sky-dive in my box
Parachuting above a beach
Then land safely on the sand
With a bowl of strawberries waiting.

Sadie Taylor (9)
Parkside Junior School, Ashbourne

The Summer Box

(Inspired by 'Magic Box' by Kit Wright)

I will put in my box . . .
The touch of the sand in-between my little toes
The fresh smell that you get from the beautiful flowers
The sweet taste of ice cream after a long tiring bike ride.

I will put in my box . . .
The first finally made daisy chain
The smell of barbecued hot dogs
The luxurious first lick of a Twister.

I will put in my box . . .
The laughing and screaming of children in the paddling pool
The scent of cut grass from the mower
The slowly swaying trees on a slightly breezy day.

I will put in my box . . .
A leafless tree in the middle of summer
A person swimming in the sand
A person sunbathing in the sea.

I will fashion my box with the shells from the sea
With ice cream inside
A breath of chocolatey goodness in ever corner.

I will search in rock pools
I will find crabs and starfish
They will talk and walk
They will play till the day is no more.

Kythe Beresford (8)
Parkside Junior School, Ashbourne

The Summer Box
(Inspired by 'Magic Box' by Kit Wright)

I will put in my box . . .
Children licking their ice creams with the tips of their tongues
Sizzling sausages on a hot barbecue on a hot day
The softness of the cat's fur against my face.

I will put in my box . . .
Children splashing in their paddling pool next door
The blueness of a fresh bottle of water from far away
Children happily raising their arms at the end of school.

I will put in my box . . .
The biggest shell off the sandy beach in Wales
The eyes of a newborn baby
The first steps of a toddler.

I will put in my box . . .
A caveman in a car
A witch on a motorbike
A squirrel on a broomstick.

My box is made of ice
The lid is made of steel
And the corners are made of a T-rex's teeth.

I shall surf in my box
On the wild Arctic waves
Then wash ashore on the icy winds
The colour of the clouds.

Leah Pedley (9)
Parkside Junior School, Ashbourne

The Summer Box
(Inspired by 'Magic Box' by Kit Wright)

I will put in my box . . .
Children playing happily in the water
Sizzling sausages burning on a barbecue
Melting ice creams running down your hand.

I will put in my box . . .
The waves crashing against the black rocks
Dad putting on suncream after he got burnt the day before
Mum and Dad laying on deckchairs whilst getting tanned.

I will put in my box . . .
Yellow sunflowers bursting out of the ground
Birds hovering over you whilst singing a song
A collection of shells with the smell of sand.

I will put in my box . . .
A kite so I can fly through the sky like a bird
A surfboard so I can charge through the waves
A friend so I can learn a new language on holiday.

My box is fashioned with silky petals picked from the fresh flowers
Fluffy clouds which have been found in the sky
Sand which has been washed up in the tide.

I shall climb in my box on the highest cliff
Then jump back down
And land in the middle of the sunlight.

Rachel Ward (9)
Parkside Junior School, Ashbourne

The Summer Box
(Inspired by 'Magic Box' by Kit Wright)

I will put in my box . . .
Bike riding on the shady Tissington trail
The lick of mint choc chip ice cream, fresh from the freezer
Cold paddling pools with splashing waves.

I will put in my box . . .
Yellow blankets of dandelions in beautiful fields
Ice cubes melting refreshingly in my mouth
Wonderful cold drinks on a hot summer's day.

I will put in my box . . .
Cats flopping out like pigs in the sun
Gardens loaded with colourful flowers
Smiling sun with sunglasses.

I will put in my box . . .
An 8th sea and a green sky
A sky-blue sun
And a bright yellow sky.

My box is fashioned from shells and ice cream
With a sand-coloured surface
And splashes of sea in the corners.

I will sunbathe in my box on golden sand
Before diving into the sea
And emerging with hundreds of shells and starfish.

Maisie Browne (8)
Parkside Junior School, Ashbourne

The Summer Box
Inspired by 'Magic Box' by Kit Wright)

I will put in my box . . .
Children playing in their colourful garden, shouting
A lick of a cold ice cream so tasty to dream
The fire of the Holy Spirit.

I will put in my box . . .
People sunbathing on the sparkling water
People sledding on the yellow sand
And grannies licking ice cream.

I will put in my box . . .
A blue squared sun
And a bright yellow sky moving
And a family setting light to a barbecue.

I will put in my box . . .
A treasure island for the summer heat
Surrounding the treasure island is glittering sparkling water
With boats rushing round.

My box is fashioned with shells
Red and orange and yellow flames
And a sprinkle of sand
I shall sunbathe on the sand
With lots of people surrounding me
And look up at the sun.

Joy Mallard (9)
Parkside Junior School, Ashbourne

My Summer Box
(Inspired by 'Magic Box' by Kit Wright)

I will put in my box . . .
Sizzling sausages roasting on a barbecue
The salty sea washing up on the beach
The touch of a freezing paddling pool.

I will put in my box . . .
A little child's laughter, playing at the park
The taste of melting milkshake in your mouth
The colour of the Sahara desert.

I will put in my box . . .
Sunny weather that makes me smile
A dream that I'm famous and sing like an angel
The beach on a really sunny day.

My box is made out of white chocolate
With gems on the lid
And a kiss from my mum in every corner
It's a special summer box.

I will climb over Mount Everest
I shall ride a special shark in my box
Then I will put a baby's first smile in my box.

I will put my box in the highest tree ever
So it's safe!

Sophie Dobson (9)
Parkside Junior School, Ashbourne

The Summer Box
(Inspired by 'Magic Box' by Kit Wright)

I will put in my box . . .
The sound of children laughing in the playground
Warmness from the sand on a beach on a holiday
Fire from the burning burgers on the barbecue.

I will put in my box . . .
The birds singing in the tree
The deep blue of a sea glistening all day
Birds flying close to the sun.

I will put in my box . . .
Lovely barbecues my dad has made
The hot floors with my bare feet
Chocolate ice cream rolling down my hand.

I will put in my box . . .
A polar bear sitting on the beach
A human in Antarctica
And a seal in a forest.

My box is fashioned from cheese, gold and silver
With moons on the lid and secrets in the middle
Its hinges are golden apples.

I shall fall in my box into a pool of Cadbury's melted chocolate
And then I will eat it all.

David Denny (9)
Parkside Junior School, Ashbourne

The Summer Box
(Inspired by 'Magic Box' by Kit Wright)

I will put in my box . . .
The tides pulling closer ashore
The sizzling sausages burning on the barbecue
The silky, soft sand in your toes.

I will put in my box . . .
The waves crashing on the big black rocks
The mouth-watering creamy ice cream
The children splashing in the rock pools.

I will put in my box . . .
Three games of volleyball on the beach
The last children playing out on a hot summer evening
The first day of a holiday.

I will put in my box . . .
A second sun and an invisible cloud
A dragon talking to the sun
A human spitting fire to a cloud.

My box is fashioned with ice cream, lollies
With suns on the lid and cones for the corners
Its hinges are made from caramelised ice creams.

I shall swim with dolphins on the coast of Florida
Then wash ashore on a yellow beach the colour of the sun.

Chloe Steeples (9)
Parkside Junior School, Ashbourne

The Summer Box
(Inspired by 'Magic Box' by Kit Wright)

I will put in my box . . .
Children swimming and dancing in the bright sun
Burning burgers and sizzling sausages
Feet being brushed on the hot prickly grass.

I will put in my box . . .
Loud giggles of happiness
Mouth-watering, delicious, juicy fruit
With shades of green everywhere.

I will put in my box . . .
The beaming hot sun of a summer's day
Peaceful dreams of happiness
Sunflowers making gardens look pretty.

I will put in my box . . .
Kangaroos bouncing in the deep snow
Polar bears padding on the hot sand.

My box is fashioned with rubies the colour of amber
With smiley faces in each corner for joy and laughter
Its hinges are made from rubber.

In my box I will visit another planet
Where aliens live and they all become my friends
Then I go out to space, the colour of dark blue eyes.

Talullah Reed (9)
Parkside Junior School, Ashbourne

The Summer Box
(Inspired by 'Magic Box' by Kit Wright)

I will put in my box . . .
The children playing at the seaside
The sizzling sausages on the barbecue
The melting ice creams.

I will put in my box . . .
The seagulls at the beach catching fish
A glass of fresh cold water
The sun shining at people.

I will put in my box . . .
The beautiful words spoken in Japanese
The laughter of people by the beach
The fish and the dolphins swimming.

I will put in my box . . .
The dark sun on a hot day
A man wearing a swimming suit out in the cold.

My box is fashioned from ice cream and ice lollies
With ice cream cones in the corners
Its hinges are lollipop sticks.

I shall eat my box in my room without the toys
Then the box comes back again
The same colour and the same shape.

Taylor Carolan (9)
Parkside Junior School, Ashbourne

The Summer Box
(Inspired by 'Magic Box' by Kit Wright)

I will put in my box . . .
The laughter when school finishes
The first barbecue of the summer
The silky waves touching my feet.

I will put in my box . . .
The camel I first saw
The first freezing ice cream
The waves crashing on the rocks.

I will put in my box . . .
A polar bear and desert
A camel in the Arctic.

I will put in my box . . .
A fifth ice cream and a black beach
A dinosaur in 2010
A person in Jurassic times.

My box is fashioned from ice cream and waves
The corners are made from camel humps
And the hinges are bicycles.

I shall surf in my box
With a giant ice cream in the Atlantic Ocean
And wash up on the shore and get attacked by a camel.

Oscar Chambers (8)
Parkside Junior School, Ashbourne

The Summer Box
(Inspired by 'Magic Box' by Kit Wright)

I will put in my box . . .
Children happily splashing in the sea having fun
Sizzling sausages burning on the barbecue
Melting ice cream running through my fingers and down my hand.

I will put in my box . . .
The waves crashing against the smooth black rocks
Dad's bad cooking after being stressed out by the heat
Children running and making sandcastles
Out of the hot, smooth sand.

I will put in my box . . .
The memory of me meeting my best friend on holiday
And playing on the beach until we had to go.

I will put in my box . . .
People sunbathing beneath the burning sun
Getting red sunburn on their backs.

My box is made from silky smooth petals
With light fluffy clouds rotating round it.

I shall fly in my box just like a kite
Soaring in the sky, looking down at the tiny people
And landing on the sea's edge looking at the horizon.

Olivia Stocks (9)
Parkside Junior School, Ashbourne

The Summer Box
(Inspired by 'Magic Box' by Kit Wright)

I will put in my box . . .
Brilliant birds swooping past the sun
Smells from a barbecue from miles away
Silky sand dancing through my toes.

I will put in my box . . .
Small, shiny seagulls pecking at the sea
The finest burgers in the world
Purple bruises from water fights.

I will put in my box . . .
A swish of a gentle breeze
Building the highest sandcastle touching the sky
Palm trees, tall and thin like matchsticks.

My box is made from swishing sand
With a sun handlebar
With carriers that have songs on
In the bottom is joy and happiness

I shall make the world's biggest candyfloss
I will dance like an angel
Then I will put my box in a dark, cold room
To rewind to the start.

Niamh Bunting (9)
Parkside Junior School, Ashbourne

My Summer Box
(Inspired by 'Magic Box' by Kit Wright)

I will put in my box . . .
A satisfying sizzling barbecue
The smell of seaside shells
The soft, smooth sand in-between my toes.

I will put in my box . . .
The bees buzzing in my back garden
The tip of a tongue touching the mouth-watering flavoured ice creams
A bright, beautiful summer yellow.

I will put in my box . . .
A blowing breeze from the high, magnificent clouds above
The dream of a peaceful walk out at night
The beaming of a sunny sunflower.

My box is made of pure gold
From an Egyptian pyramid with sprinkled sugar in the corners
It is magical and my secret summer hide-out.

I shall surf on the wonderful waters of the Eastern Lake
I will climb over the marvellous rainbow
Then I will put my box on my bedside table
So that every night I can creep into my special summer box.

Phoebe Hannah Barks (9)
Parkside Junior School, Ashbourne

The Summer Box
(Inspired by 'Magic Box' by Kit Wright)

I will put in my box . . .
Children smiling and having fun
Smell of sizzling sausages on a perfect day
The sensation of cold water cooling me down.

I will put in my box . . .
Tweeting birds hovering by
Sweet, succulent strawberry ice cream dancing on my taste buds
Red devilish flowers blooming on the trees.

I will put in my box . . .
Nice hot summer weather
A dream of flying into the deep blue sky
Sun reflecting on the blue water.

My box is fashioned from ice
With sparkling stars on the lid
And nails of a dragon's toes on the corners
It is very special.

I shall swim in the nice, cooling, blue water
I will also dance under the bright sun
Then I will put my box on an everlasting tree
So no one can reach it.

Divine Yu (9)
Parkside Junior School, Ashbourne

The Summer Box
(Inspired by 'Magic Box' by Kit Wright)

I will put in my box . . .
Children swimming and dancing in the bright sun
Burning burgers and sizzling sausages
Warm, hot, prickly grass on your feet.

I will put in my box . . .
Loud giggles of happiness
Mouth-watering delicious, juicy fruit
A light blue sea washing away dark green seaweed.

I will put in my box . . .
A hot, bright sun shining on me
Peaceful dreams of happiness
Birds tweeting in the tall green tree.

My box is made from kids' happiness on holiday
With smiley faces on the lid and secrets in the corners
It's covered with bright yellow stars and pink flowers.

I shall swim in the light blue sea
I will walk the warm yellow sand on the big beach
Then I will put my box on the beach
Because it is good to let it float away
And I want the things to come true.

Jordan Titterton (9)
Parkside Junior School, Ashbourne

The Summer Box
(Inspired by 'Magic Box' by Kit Wright)

I will put in my box . . .
The sparkling stars from a summer night
The smell of sizzling sausages on a brilliant barbecue
The touch of water from the cold sea.

I will put in my box . . .
The laughing of happy children playing in the sand
The taste of beefy burgers from the grill
I will put a beam of yellow from the sun in my box.

I will put in my box . . .
I will put in a hot summer day
A dream of being a chocolate bear, melting in the hot summer sun
Daisies growing in the light green grass.

My box is fashioned from sun-hot sand
With summer seashells on the lid
It is the best box in the universe.

I shall surf in my box
I will play beach volleyball too
Then I will put my box in a secret place
That only I know about
And keep it just for me.

Faith Roberts (9)
Parkside Junior School, Ashbourne

The Summer Box
(Inspired by 'Magic Box' by Kit Wright)

I will put in my box . . .
The sea waving about and crashing against the rocks
The barbecue burning sausages
The soft petals of a flower, like a pillow.

I will put in my box . . .
Children screaming with happiness and laughter
A delicious Victoria sponge
Golden yellow roses like the sun.

I will put in my box . . .
The sun glittering up in the sky
Climbing the tallest red sunflowers
Daisies growing rapidly like a genie.

My box is made of a sun
With a barbecue as the lid and sunflowers in the corners
Its hinges are sausages.

I will swim in the swimming pool
And build a colossal sandcastle
Then I will put my box on the beach
Because it is a summer box.

Cain Belcher White (9)
Parkside Junior School, Ashbourne

The Summer Box
(Inspired by 'Magic Box' by Kit Wright)

I will put in my box . . .
Three bright yellow dandelions swishing beautifully
The smell of sizzling sausages
The swish of fresh summer hitting your face.

I will put in my box . . .
The sweet twitter of birds singing
The taste of hot chocolate burning my mouth
The shade of blue in the midday sky.

I will put in my box . . .
The sunshine shining in my eyes
The dream of walking with my dog
Soft sand lying on the beach.

My box is made from pure gold
With stars all over the lid
It is finished with bees in the corners.

I shall sing in my box
I will dance in my box
Then I will put my box on top of my highest shelf
Where it's safe.

Courtney Thorpe (8)
Parkside Junior School, Ashbourne

77

The Summer Box
(Inspired by 'Magic Box' by Kit Wright)

I will put in my box . . .
Flowers sprouting on a summer morning
Sausages sizzling on a barbecue at lunchtime
The silky sand on a beach in France.

I will put in my box . . .
Children laughing in the red-hot sun
The salt of the summer sea
The blue of the sky on a clear day.

I will put in my box . . .
The summer sun on a burning day
The sun gleaming down at me
A waterfall crashing on the rocks below.

My box is made of molten rock, red-hot from the sun
With sunflowers on the lid
It is the hottest thing on Earth.

I shall water-ski in my box
I will rock climb in my box
Then I will put my box under a floorboard
So no one can get it.

Samuel Moore (8)
Parkside Junior School, Ashbourne

The Summer Box
(Inspired by 'Magic Box' by Kit Wright)

I will put in my box . . .
Bright yellow dandelions glowing like a rocket blasting off
The sense of Cadbury's chocolate melting in the sun
The touch of golden sand sizzling under my toes.

I will put in my box . . .
The sound of bees buzzing loudly in the sky
The taste of chilled ice cream melting in your mouth
The shade of bright yellow, beaming like the sun.

I will put in my box . . .
The sunny weather of the summertime sun
The dream of happiness spreading around the world
A flower growing in the swishing grass.

My box is made from shimmering sand
With dandelions and buttercups in the corners and on the lid
Its hinges are made from shiny rocks.

I shall play in my box in scorching hot weather
I will swim in my box
Then I shall put my box in a room
Nice and cool for it to cool down.

Henry Pearson (8)
Parkside Junior School, Ashbourne

The Summer Box
(Inspired by 'Magic Box' by Kit Wright)

I will put in my box . . .
The multicoloured summer fruits sitting on the market stall
The smell of freshly mowed grass wafting round my garden
The tip of a tongue touching an ice cream.

I will put in my box . . .
A tweeting bird up in its nest
Burning sand wriggling through my toes
The colour turquoise to remind me of the sea.

I will put in my box . . .
Snow falling on a summer's day
The dream of summer never ending
Lush, green summer leaves ready to fall.

My box is fashioned from bluebells and daisies
With rays of sun on the lid and good times in the corners
And its hinges are blades from the bottom of a surfboard.

I shall paint in my box
I will climb in my box
Then I will put my box in a secret place
So no one can find it.

Ellen Richmond (8)
Parkside Junior School, Ashbourne

My Summer Box
(Inspired by 'Magic Box' by Kit Wright)

I will put in my box . . .
Freshly mowed grass in the shining sunshine
The scent of sizzling sausages on a barbecue
The touch of soft sand between your toes.

I will put in my box . . .
The sound of sea splashing on the beach
The taste of a tongue licking a lolly
The colour of green grass.

I will put in my box . . .
Scorching sun on the beach
The dream of everlasting summer holidays
A fox searching for its prey.

My box is made from pure gold and tree bark
With sharp thorns and pine needles on the lid
It's decorated with bright, smooth stones.

I shall sunbathe in my box on a sandy beach
I will climb a scorching tree and slide down
Then I will put my box in a secret tree house
So that it will be safe forever.

Tommi Greville (8)
Parkside Junior School, Ashbourne

The Summer Box
(Inspired by 'Magic Box' by Kit Wright)

I will put in my box . . .
Flying butterflies everywhere
The fragrance of freshly mown grass
Brilliant beefburgers burning on the barbecue.

I will put in my box . . .
Whistling wind blowing through weeping willows
The mouth-watering milkshake melting in your mouth
The pink sky from a setting sun.

I will put in my box . . .
The hot sun blazing beautifully from dawn till dusk
The dream of riding a horse
A gushing waterfall smashing through the rocks.

My box is made from glittering golden spiders webs
With chocolate stars in the middle
It is the most beautiful box ever made.

I shall ride a horse round a track
I shall swim all around the oceans
I shall hide my box in the tree house
Where no one will find it.

Abbi Daughtry (8)
Parkside Junior School, Ashbourne

The Summer Box
(Inspired by 'Magic Box' by Kit Wright)

I will put in my box . . .
The shimmering sun
Fresh flowers already done
The first splash of a swimming pool.

I will put in my box . . .
Beautiful birds twittering all day
Brilliant burgers ready to eat
And a yellow brighter than the sun.

I will put in my box . . .
The sunniest Saturday
A never-ending summer day
And lots of beautiful bushes.

My box is made from the first summer grass
With sunflower seeds in all four corners
Its hinges are made from sizzling sausages.

I shall paddle in my box
Then I will sunbathe all day
I will put my box inside an old oak tree
Away from everybody except me.

Oliver Massey (9)
Parkside Junior School, Ashbourne

The Summer Box
(Inspired by 'Magic Box' by Kit Wright)

I will put in my box . . .
Weeping willows gently swaying in the breeze
Freshly mown grass in the meadows
The rough rocks rolling into the soft sandy sea.

I will put in my box . . .
Birds singing in the early morning
Mouth-watering milkshake melting in my mouth
The roaring red of an England shirt.

I will put in my box . . .
Blazing hot sun from dawn until dusk
My winning goal for England in the World Cup
Fish flickering through the gushing water.

My box is made from a shiny golden spider's web
With silver tractor wheels for a lid
And corners made of bronze stars.

I shall fly over the fluffy white clouds
Landing in the biggest tree house
Where I shall hide my precious box
So that only the moon and stars can see it.

Matthew Bacon (9)
Parkside Junior School, Ashbourne

The Summer Box

(Inspired by 'Magic Box' by Kit Wright)

I will put in my box . . .
Buzzing bumblebees flying past
The smell of sizzling smoked sausages
The touch of soft sand between my toes.

I will put in my box . . .
Loud music drifting through the air
Strawberries with sugar, juicing in my mouth
I will add light blue, like the sky.

I will put in my box . . .
A blazing sun
The dream of an Olympic runner
I will put in a hedgehog.

I will make my box from emeralds
The lid is made from silver
It is decorated with neon lights.

I will eat strawberries in my box
I will also run in my box
I will put my box in my room
So that I can visit whenever I want.

John Armstrong (9)
Parkside Junior School, Ashbourne

My Summer Box
(Inspired by 'Magic Box' by Kit Wright)

I will put in my box . . .
A shimmering, shining swimming pool bubbling and churning
The bold smell of thyme and lime
The soft sand creeping through my toes.

I will put in my box . . .
The screeching and roaring of an F1 car tearing up the track
Supple summer strawberry surprise flooding my mouth with taste
A minty green, the colour of the grass.

I will put in my box . . .
A hot summer's day baking a cake in its own heat
A dream of having a resort island with my cat
A spring hedgehog snuffling around.

My box is fashioned from light and titanium and heat
With sparks on the lid and sand in the corners
The hinges are coral from the coral reef.

I shall swing through the trees like a monkey
Throw a barbecue with my friends
I will keep my box perched on the edge of the universe
Where only I can reach it.

Benton Stevens (9)
Parkside Junior School, Ashbourne

The Summer Box
(Inspired by 'Magic Box' by Kit Wright)

I will put in my box . . .
Flying butterflies fluttering everywhere
The fragrance of sizzling sausages
Brilliant beefburgers burning on the barbecue.

I will put in my box . . .
Birds singing in the early morning
Mouth-watering milkshake melting in your mouth
The pinky-orange sky from a setting sun.

I will put in my box . . .
Blazing hot sun from dawn until dusk
The dream of being in the England team and winning the World Cup
A snuffling hedgehog shuffling along in search of slimy worms.

My box is made of glittery gorgeous gold
The corners are made of sparkly stars all around
It is the most precious box ever.

I shall race against Morgan in my box
I will win every time
Then I will put my box in a tractor
So that farmers can look in my box.

Jade Jones (9)
Parkside Junior School, Ashbourne

The Summer Box
(Inspired by 'Magic Box' by Kit Wright)

I will put in my box . . .
The mouth-watering, sizzling sausages
The ice-cold ice cream launching down my stomach
The burning, spicy, hot fajitas.

I will put in my box . . .
The beautiful flowers growing gracefully
The children playing on the hot, wonderful beach
The children having a big water fight on the street.

I will put in my box . . .
The waves swishing, bashing the rocks
Everyone boogying on a hot boiling day to the loud music
The ocean sea roaring.

My box is made from quivering diamonds reflecting the sun
With dinosaur teeth poking out the corners
It is shiny as the world.

I shall skateboard to California by gliding all the way
I will surf to Atlantis with the wild breeze through my hair
Then I will put my box under my bed
Because no one looks under my bed and it's safe.

Joe Nightingale (9)
Parkside Junior School, Ashbourne

The Summer Box
(Inspired by 'Magic Box' by Kit Wright)

I will put in my box . . .
People laughing and having fun in the sparkling pool
The smell of sizzling sausages and beefy burgers
The after-sun cooling your warm sunburn.

I will put in my box . . .
The laughter of playing children
The taste of freezing cold ice cream
I will put a swirl of light violet.

I will put in my box . . .
The sun shining on me
Riding on my horse all day in the sun
Seeing the wonderful buttercups.

My box is made of sand off the beach
With daisies for corners
It is the best box in the world.

I shall surf on my box
I will fly in the blue sky
Then I will store it somewhere secret
And keep it safe.

Sophie French (9)
Parkside Junior School, Ashbourne

The Summer Box
(Inspired by 'Magic Box' by Kit Wright)

I will put in my box . . .
Birds flying high in the light blue sky
Sizzling sausages on a tasty barbecue
The delicate breeze flowing in my face.

I will put in my box . . .
Birds swiftly tweeting as they fly by
A freezing cold toffee milkshake
Purple flowers blooming everywhere.

I will put in my box . . .
The sunniest sun in the deep blue sky
A dream of flying high in the sky
The sun reflecting on the deep blue sea.

My box is fashioned with ice cream
And milkshakes in the corners
It is the best box in the world.

I shall sunbathe on the sunniest beach
I will surf on the bluest water
Then I will put my box in the tallest tree
Where everyone can see it.

Bethany Hemsil (9)
Parkside Junior School, Ashbourne

My Summer's Box
(Inspired by 'Magic Box' by Kit Wright)

I will put in my box . . .
The sparkling stars of a summer's night
The smell of beefy burgers on a barbecue
A touch of blossom on a tall tree.

I will put in my box . . .
The sound of birds tweeting on a summer's morning
The taste of toffee milkshake melting in my mouth
I would put bright yellow in my box.

I will put in my box . . .
A scorching hot day with no rain
A dream of England winning the World Cup
And a big oak tree growing on a summer's day.

My box is made from seaside rocks and sand in the corners
It is the best box you can have.

I shall surf in my box
And I will play beach volleyball in my box
Then I will put my box up high on a shelf
Away from brothers and cousins.

Calum Richardson (9)
Parkside Junior School, Ashbourne

The Summer Box
(Inspired by 'Magic Box' by Kit Wright)

The spherical, boiling sun, glittering silver sparks
The sizzling barbecue smoke crackling across the fence
The burning hot sand creeping between your toes.

I will put in my box . . .
The buzzing bees hovering over a flower
A crispy ice cream cone being crunched noisily
A touch of light blue water being put in a freezer.

I will put in my box . . .
A fresh, breezy summer morning
A wish about playing all night long
The shimmering silver water in a pure pond of legend.

My box is made from summer flowers sewn together
With my wish in the corner and sunshine on the lid
Its hinges are made from magical cockleshells.

I shall bodyboard in my box . . .
I will then land on a mysterious island
I will put my box in the corner of the universe
Because I want to keep it safe forever.

Holly Herring (9)
Parkside Junior School, Ashbourne

The Summer Box
(Inspired by 'Magic Box' by Kit Wright)

I will put in my box . . .
A boat bathing on the shallow seashore
A hot-air balloon
A pair of swimming shorts.

I will put in my box . . .
A ringmaster with a swimming suit
And a diver with a top hat
An ice cream van that gives ice for free.

I will put in my box . . .
Seagulls squawking
Waves going *swoosh*
Children laughing on land, sea and air.

I will put in my box . . .
22 dogs and 3 puppies sleeping in my caravan
A last lifeguard's save
And a first wave, waving, 'Hello!'

I will put in my box . . .
Care, love, goodness and humour.

Samuel Morris (9)
Parkside Junior School, Ashbourne

The Summer Box
(Inspired by 'Magic Box' by Kit Wright)

I will put in my box . . .
Ice cream, a delicious thing to smell and dream
The touch of the freezing cold water when the ice melts
The nip of a bottle of fizz on a summer's day.

I will put in my box . . .
The sight of camels and kangaroos on the scorching sand
The taste of an ice-cold ice lolly
The gentle sound of the water in the paddling pool.

I will put in my box
The colour yellow
The colour blue
The colour turquoise.

I will fashion my box with daisies
The hinges will be made of bees
The lid will be yellow.

I will water-ski in my box
I will bounce off the end
I will splash in the water.

Callum Pattinson (9)
Parkside Junior School, Ashbourne

The Summer Box
(Inspired by 'Magic Box' by Kit Wright)

I will put in my box . . .
The smooth, hot sand on my toes
The children laughing in the bright sunshine
The smell of ice cream.

I will put in my box . . .
People sky-diving out of a plane
The scream of people screaming
The yellow of the bright, sandy beach.

I will put in my box . . .
The bright sunshine
The dream of cruising on a boat
The bright shine on the dandelions.

My box is made from sand
With shells as hinges and it's colourful.

I shall sky-dive out of a plane
I will sunbathe on my box
Then I will put in my box waves, sand and deckchairs.

Zachery Maher (9)
Parkside Junior School, Ashbourne

The Summer Box
(Inspired by 'Magic Box' by Kit Wright)

I will put in my box . . .
Bumblebees buzzing
Beefburgers on a barbecue
The soft sand squishing between my toes.

I will put in my box . . .
The sound of children laughing happily
Big beefburgers
Ocean blue droplets.

I will put in my box . . .
Beaming sunshine glistening down
Icy cold ice cream
Birds fluttering about.

My box is made from glistening gold
And shiny with glimmering gold
I shall surf in my box
I shall fly around the world seven times.

Joseph Jordan (9)
Parkside Junior School, Ashbourne

The Summer Box
(Inspired by 'Magic Box' by Kit Wright)

I will put in my box . . .
A swimming pool full of lemonade
And children sunbathing on a beautiful beach
A football in a long, wide footy field.

I will put in my box . . .
A man surfing on the highest wave
A ginormous park that everyone can enjoy.

I will put in my box . . .
A famous rock band singing my favourite song
Fireworks heading towards the super hot sun.

My box is made of wood
And has a lock to keep it safe
And also has a rock eagle on top
And has my name in bubble writing.

Sean Likeman (9)
Parkside Junior School, Ashbourne

The Summer Box
(Inspired by 'Magic Box' by Kit Wright)

I will put in my box . . .
The soft touch of sand from the beach
The sweet smell of the sea
A beautiful sand wave
And excellent water trees.

I will put in my box . . .
The sweet smell of blossom trees
The sweet taste of apple grass
I will snorkel in my box and build a sandcastle.

My box is made out of water and sand and ice cream.

Macie Hindley (9)
Parkside Junior School, Ashbourne

The Summer Box
(Inspired by 'Magic Box' by Kit Wright)

I can smell a hot dog on the barbecue
Honey smell of flowers
Salty sea
Suncream rubbed on my skin.

I can hear the waves like wind
Birds twittering in the trees
I can see the sea and the sun
So I can see the sun blowing hot and cold
Colourful flowers and soft grass.

I can touch the sea and the sandcastle
And the shells
I can taste chocolate cake
And a biscuit and hot chocolate
And super ice cream, fresh iced juice.

Weronika Rogowska (8)
Parkside Junior School, Ashbourne

The Summer Box
(Inspired by 'Magic Box' by Kit Wright)

I will put in my box . . .
The sight of a shark
The tasty sweet fruit
The sound of birds singing.

I will put in my box . . .
Children laughing in a pool
The taste of juicy apples
The smell of ice cream from the air.

I will put in my box . . .
A sunny day
A ship flying in the sky
A plane underwater
A cheetah running for its life.

Xander Wilkinson (9)
Parkside Junior School, Ashbourne

The Summer Box
(Inspired by 'Magic Box' by Kit Wright)

I will put in my box . . .
The lick of ice cream tasting of strawberry beer and chocolate mint
Children having fun in the bright sunny sunshine
The yellow dandelions as far as I can see.

I will put in my box . . .
A cold glass of water I drink
Children having a ride in the park and being happy
Sandy beach being shone on by the hot sun.

I will put in my box . . .
Children having water fights in their back gardens.

My box will be made of strong card or paper.

Harry Collins (8)
Parkside Junior School, Ashbourne

The Summer Box
(Inspired by 'Magic Box' by Kit Wright)

I will put in my box . . .
The smooth, soft, yellow sand
With big shifting tides
Sky-divers landing in a field with dandelions
Children licking luscious ice creams with flakes.

I will put in my box . . .
People sunbathing with a splash of suncream
People making castles out of shells.

My box is made from leather
With a sun on the lid
And deckchairs on the corners.

Luke Michael Ayres (9)
Parkside Junior School, Ashbourne

I Am Speaking For . . .

I am speaking for the rainforests
that are being destroyed by the fires.

I am speaking for the birds that are having their nests cut down.

I am speaking for the puzzled animals that are constantly
running away from the flames.

I am speaking for the rivers that are being polluted by our waste.

I am speaking for the rainforests that are dying for our enjoyment.

I am speaking for the rainforests that are being cut down for
McDonald's to ranch their cattle.

I am speaking for the rainforests that are dying out.

I am speaking for the starving tribes that are losing their lives.

I am speaking for to *you!* You are forcing *everything out!*

Ronan Curtis (10)
Parkwood Primary School, Scunthorpe

What They Deserve

I am speaking for
the animals that are
abused in ways you
can't imagine.

I am speaking for
animals that are
dehydrated and hungry.

I am speaking for
the cats and dogs
that are kept in small
cages.

I am speaking for
the chickens that
are forced to lay
eggs.

I am speaking for
the animals that
are emaciated
because of their
cold-hearted
owners.

I am speaking for
the animals that wonder
what they've done.
How would you feel if it were you?
Just think about that.

Devon James (10)
Parkwood Primary School, Scunthorpe

Roller Coasters

Sitting on a roller coaster
thinking it might be fun
my heart might stop pounding
when the ride is done.

Staring at the station
gathering up speed
a good-feeling massage
is what I really need.

Twisting and turning
feeling really sick
screaming and shouting
and so is Rick.

As we go up and down
and round and round
me and Rick
are now feeling really sick.

When the ride has some to a stop
our legs all wobbly, our hands like a spinning top
I am pleased the roller coaster's come to a stop
I won't ride that ride again
It is a ride I will not forget.

Harry Tindall (10)
Parkwood Primary School, Scunthorpe

Trains

Trains are purple, blue and green
Steam engines can be seen
Electrics and diesels on the line
I think one of them should be mine.

Maizii Wells (9)
Parkwood Primary School, Scunthorpe

I Am Speaking For . . .

I am speaking for the dog's owners to stop pushing this dog away.

I am speaking for the emaciated dog,
who is battered nearly to the point of death.

I am speaking for the poor dog that must be thinking,
Why me?

I am speaking for all the battered animal out there.

I am speaking for the animals that are thinking,
Why do I deserve this?

I am speaking for the brutally beaten dog.

I am speaking for the RSPCA to stop animals
getting to the point of death.

I am speaking for the dog's owners to
stop abusing this wonderful animal.

I am speaking to the owners to treat the dog in a non-painful way.

I am speaking for the RSPCA to love and care for this dog.

I am speaking for the owners to stop
this horrible game they're playing!

Ryan Boult (11)
Parkwood Primary School, Scunthorpe

I'm Speaking For . . .

I am speaking for all that animals that are mistreated and starved by their abusive owners.

I am speaking for the questioning dog, that thinks,
Why me? What have I done to deserve this pain?

I am speaking for the dog that is abused in ways
you could never imagine, all day, every day.

I am speaking for the dog that is haunted by its owner.

I am speaking for all those animals
that are scared to go back to their hell-home.

I am speaking for the horse that is emaciated.

I am speaking for all the sadly abused animals
that are close to death.

I am speaking for the dog that's scared of its own shadow.

I am speaking for all the animals that are still being abused,
right next door to you!

I am speaking to all the owners who are neglecting these animals,
when they don't know how it feels to be treated this way.

Kayley Grice (10)
Parkwood Primary School, Scunthorpe

I Am Speaking

I am speaking for the dog that thinks he's worthless,
has no home to go to at night.

I am speaking for the dog that is abused
by his stone-hearted owner.

I am speaking for the dog that is emaciated, no food,
Why has it come to this?

I am speaking for the dog that is frightened about what's to happen.

I am speaking for the dog, that is vulnerable, scared of his owner's
shadow.

I am speaking for the dog who has done nothing,
Why am I here?

I am speaking for the dog who was getting bored and who had no
one to play with.

I am speaking to the owner who is never bothered.

I am speaking for all the animals that are puzzled,
Why me?

James Mullen (10)
Parkwood Primary School, Scunthorpe

I Am Speaking

I am speaking for the dog that has been mistreated,
That was emaciated, abused and starved.

I am speaking for the dog which is confused and is puzzled,
Why is he doing this to me?

I am speaking for the dog which has been locked up.

I am speaking for the people that are being cruel to the animals.

Stop it!

Lewis Snowden (11)
Parkwood Primary School, Scunthorpe

I Am Speaking For The Dog . . .

I am speaking for the dog who is puzzled, *why me?*

I am speaking for the dog who is frightened of what his owner's going to do next.

I am speaking for the dog that has been neglected by his cold-hearted owner.

I am speaking for the dog that is vulnerable because of all his owner's horrid powers.

I am speaking for the dog that is emaciated to the bone.

I am speaking for the dog who is threatened by his horrible conditions.

I am speaking for the unloved dog that has an unloving owner.

I am speaking for the dog that is haunted by his owner's shadow.

I am speaking for the dog that has never has a luscious bone.

Mark my words, this is a dangerous game you are playing.
When they find you they will get you.

Nikita Wells (10)
Parkwood Primary School, Scunthorpe

I Am Speaking

I am speaking for the dog that has been neglected by his owner and locked in a small room.

I am speaking for the dog that thinks every night,
What have I done to deserve this cruel punishment?

I am speaking for the dog that might be lucky to eat once a week.

I am speaking for the dog that wonders
what will happen next night.

I am speaking for all dogs that have been abused.

Joe Gibson (10)
Parkwood Primary School, Scunthorpe

I Am Speaking For . . .

I am speaking for the dog who is neglected all day, every day.

I am speaking for the cat who is kept on a chain,
he has to live in his own waste.

I am speaking for the wild animals that are kept in small, enclosed
spaces.
Why? They should be out in the wild.

I am speaking for the dog who is abused in ways
you could not imagine.

I am speaking for the reptiles who are kept in small tanks
that are never cleaned.

I am speaking for the horse who is unloved and kept on a lead.

I am speaking for the fish that has never had clean water.

I am speaking for the dog who has never had fresh water to drink.

I am speaking for all the animals that are mistreated.
Why?

Jessica Deighton (11)
Parkwood Primary School, Scunthorpe

Animals

Animals are beautiful,
loving and always wanting to play,
there are big animals,
small animals,
fat animals,
thin animals,
nice animals,
like the dogs for the blind
and the animals that are really nasty
and bite your behind!

Yasmin Dawson (10)
Parkwood Primary School, Scunthorpe

Save The Animals

I am speaking for the starving animals chained to a post or something else. They are emaciated, confused, scared and vulnerable.

I am speaking for the dog, that was scarred on the face and starved, but saved by the RSPCA.

I am speaking for the horse who was definitely emaciated because you could see his ribs, starved almost to death.

I am speaking for the battery chickens, trapped in coops, forced to lay eggs.

I am speaking for the poor fish, swimming in toxic and radioactive rivers.

Mark my words, we will be the only animals left on Earth if this keeps happening.
So don't be cruel, be nice
Or else!

Ashley Gouldthorpe (11)
Parkwood Primary School, Scunthorpe

I Am Speaking

I am speaking for the dog that is mistreated:
What have I done to deserve this?

I am speaking for the animals that have been emaciated.

I am speaking for the cold-hearted owners of these poor animals.

I am speaking for the dogs that get abused every day.

I am speaking for all the starving animals.

I am speaking for the dog who is distressed.

I am speaking for the owners
who couldn't be bothered to feed their pets.

I am speaking for all the animals that are still being starved,
all over the world.

Ben Jacklin (10)
Parkwood Primary School, Scunthorpe

Milly Billy

Milly Billy likes to eat
Something silly is so sweet
Pumpkin pie with golden syrup
Hmm, lovely, lovely, Milly Billy.

Milly Billy likes to eat
Something silly is so sweet
Chocolate trifle
With a teaspoon of honey
Yummy, lovely, yummy, Milly Billy

Milly Billy likes to eat
Something silly is so sweet
Ice cream and chocolate sauce,
Tasty, lovely, yummy, tasty Milly Billy.

Kaylee Walker (8)
Parkwood Primary School, Scunthorpe

Silly Milly

Silly Milly likes to eat
Anything sweet is her favourite treat.
Sticky, licky ice lollies,
Mm! Sticky, licky Silly Milly.

Silly Milly likes to eat
Anything sweet is her favourite treat
Bouncy honey bears
Mm! Sticky, licky, bouncy Silly Milly.

Silly Milly likes to eat
Anything sweet is her favourite treat
Sweet cream cake,
Yum, mm!
Sticky, licky, bouncy Silly Milly.

Bethany Callaghan (9)
Parkwood Primary School, Scunthorpe

I Am Speaking For . . .

I am speaking for the dog who is frightened to go back home.

I am speaking for the dog who is puzzled,
He is thinking,
What have I done wrong, to deserve this?

I am speaking for the dog who is unloved.

I am speaking for the dog who is lonely,
I have no one to care for me.

I am speaking for the dog who is useless,
I have no strength to care anymore.

I am speaking for the dog who is starving.

I am speaking for all the animals who are about to die.

Courtney Knudssen (11)
Parkwood Primary School, Scunthorpe

I Am Speaking For . . .

I am speaking for those trees, in the rainforest, that are getting chopped down and being killed by ignorant and self-thinking people.

I am speaking for the tribes who are being kicked out of their homes.

I am speaking for the animals which are being killed and forced to leave their own homes.

I am speaking for the loggers who are doing their job for money to feed their families.

You will all die unhappy, what have the rainforests done to deserve this kind of behaviour?

Fraser Bramley (10)
Parkwood Primary School, Scunthorpe

Baby Animals

Baby animals are cute and sometimes cuddly,
If anybody thinks not,
They must be just around the plot.
A baby foal opens its eyes
As its mum, friends and family
Come to greet it.
The little puppy squirms and wriggles,
As its mum licks its fur clean.
The little pigs go *oink, oink, oink,*
Whilst the youngest one squeals and tries to stand up.
But most of all the baby animals
All around the world
Are very important to us humans.
So we should take care of them
As long as we can!

Sophie Camp (11)
Rosliston CE Primary School, Swadlincote

Evie Grace

I have an aunty Nicola
And an Uncle Stu
They went to the hospital
For child number 2

She waited for hours
Until quarter to four
Next thing she knew
The doctor's at the door

In came the doctor
In came the nurse
In came the surgeon
They washed their hands first

Out popped my cousin
With a cough and a cry
To meet her mum and dad
With a tear in their eyes

In ran her brother Tom
With his grandad and his nan
In ran the family
With presents in their hands

I've got a little cousin
Her name is Evie Grace
We went to the hospital
To see her little face.

Lily D'Avila (10)
St John's CE Primary School, Worksop

The Violent Sea

The sea was calm
when they set sail,
then it went furious,
like a killer whale.

Further on it all went silent,
next thing you know
it all went violent.

Like a wolf,
the wind was howling,
the Stella started growling.

The waves were huge,
they were so high,
all of a sudden
they reached the sky.

The boat was rocking,
side to side,
it was so dangerous,
we had to hide.

They looked for us,
it all went quiet,
we didn't have to hide,
it was only a little tide.

Taylor Thackery (11)
St John's CE Primary School, Worksop

Storm At Sea

As the storm came closer
The rain began to pour.
Waves crashing on the boat,
Like an angry lion's roar.

A lightning flash struck the boat,
Now it can hardly float.
People screaming everywhere,
For a lifeboat, but they aren't there.

I heard the ship's bell ring,
Scared people heard a ping.
The giant mast began to fall,
This wasn't funny at all.

The storm clouds began to clear,
I saw an island, it was near.
I suddenly thought of home,
But there I was, all alone.

Waves are huge,
Trying to flood the ship.
Lightning flashing,
Thunder roaring,
Tops of the waves are like horses galloping.

Jasmine Fox (11)
St John's CE Primary School, Worksop

Storm At Sea

It's a crashing storm,
Wind howling like a wolf,
Sky as dark as a cave.

Lightning, shaped like a fork,
The boat rocking like a broken cradle,
Dogs barking in fright,
Gulls squawking in the light.
It's such a fright.

Many people think it's a fight,
From land all you can see
Is lightning breaking free
Black clouds like lead
And waves towering up ahead.

Boats are creaking,
Gulls are screaming,
Above the screaming,
In light the bell is gleaming.
Now it's calming down,
Maybe I won't drown.

Cameron Preece (11)
St John's CE Primary School, Worksop

Storm At Sea

Storm getting closer
rain starting to fall
I suddenly see a flash
then I hear a bang.

Waves getting angry
crashing down on the water.
Storm!

Sam Baker (10)
St John's CE Primary School, Worksop

Fairy Tale

There was once a little fairy,
Her real name was Mary.
She lived in a house
With her little pet mouse.
She played by the stream
Where she would often dream.
But when she awoke,
She thought she saw smoke.
It was smoke from the stream,
She said, 'I lost my mouse, or so it would seem.'
Then the mouse came running up to her side,
He said, 'I've found a good place to hide.'
Off they went into the trees,
While the mouse was nibbling on his cheese.
There they were, all happy and smiling,
When they came across a girl called Miley.
Miley had on a colourful bandanna,
Just like magic she turned into Hannah Montana.

Ellie-May Wesley (10)
St John's CE Primary School, Worksop

The Storm

Storm brings thunder, storm brings lightning,
Rocking boats on mile-high waves,
That not even the bravest sailor dare brave.
As lightning strikes and thunder booms,
People on ships lock themselves in their room.

Waves rising out of the sea,
Like a giant mouth opening up to eat another ship.
It's always hungry, crashing against ships,
Fighting for a meal.

Tom Webster (11)
St John's CE Primary School, Worksop

Chocolate Is The Best

Chocolate is the best sensation
It really is a great temptation
KitKat, Crunchie, Twirl and more
They always get the perfect score.

I like it hot, I like it cold
But I don't like it covered in mould
Lindt chocolate bunny
It tastes so scrummy.

Rosy-pink mice
They are really nice
Chocolate eggs with buttons inside
When I get one I certainly don't mind
Why buy diamonds and jewels
When you can buy a packet of Revels?

Darcey Frances (11)
St John's CE Primary School, Worksop

Storm At Sea

It was all calm when the waves turned bad.
Everyone was so sad.
Waves, like white, galloping horses,
Thunder sounds like washing machines,
Waves sky-high,
The sky dark and dull.

Under the moon danger is around the corner,
A light in the distance soon disappears,
Everyone goes in fear,
Rain hits the ocean with a really heavy motion.

Waves are an angry beast.

Jessica Martin (11)
St John's CE Primary School, Worksop

The Ferocious Sea

The waves were calm, no sound to be heard,
The calmness turned to panic, the silence turned to thunder,
The bright blue sky soon turned to black,
The waves were gushing forward and back.
The sea as fast as a cheetah, lightning as bright as the sun.

The ferocious waves as large as a bear,
The white froth like galloping horses,
Pitter-patter, pitter-patter,

Whoosh,swish, whoosh, swish went the fierce waves.

As the big black clouds faded away
The bright blue sky came back.
Everything went clam again
And the sea went still - until next time.

Olivia Victoria Moody & Emily Twible
St John's CE Primary School, Worksop

The Storm

Waves crashing against the rocks
In the distance you can see the old, rusty docks
The waves so tall
The waves so high
Pure white moon, as round as a spoon
The sky is grim
The sea is angry
The sky is grey
So is the bay
Black clouds above you
Blue sea beneath you.

Robert Wordingham (11)
St John's CE Primary School, Worksop

Storm At Sea

Thunder is loud
There's a black cloud

Lightning dashes
As the lighthouse flashes

Waves are crashing
Lightning is flashing

The wind is howling
Stella, the dog is howling!

Alex Lockwood (11)
St John's CE Primary School, Worksop

The Seven Seas

The sun has gone, it isn't shining,
Devils throw spears of lightning.
They seem to come in perfect timing.

The horses guide their fiercest friends,
But just until the darkness ends,
The angry thunder booms and bangs.

The horses died, they've gone away,
The sun's back out, it's a lovely day!

Emily Wright (11)
St John's CE Primary School, Worksop

Sea Curse

S harks gliding, dolphins hiding,
E ager horses on the waves, leaping onto the sand, catching prey,
A bove the dark, gloomy sky a curse is awaiting.

C urses, curses
U nder the sea, round the corner waiting for me.
R aindrops, raindrops, rainstorm waiting for me,
S trong sea waves crashing against the howling wind,
E verlasting storm, never to be seen again.

Courtney Watkinson (11)
St John's CE Primary School, Worksop

Storm Ahead

Waves crashing, Stella howling,
As he's under the table growling,
Sails flapping fast and high.

Black clouds getting angry,
Sat on the boat, really hungry,
Pots and pans starting to bang like thunder,
Get my umbrella up, starts to rain,
So I go under.

Laura Ordidge (11)
St John's CE Primary School, Worksop

Storm At Sea

As the old sails flapped in the gusting winds,
Lightning like forks hitting the blue seas,
Thunder like drums, spreading around the fearless land,
Huge, black clouds followed me all the way,
Slowly, slowly it clears once again,
But it won't be long till next time.

Laura Simmen (11)
St John's CE Primary School, Worksop

The Old Lady Who Did Karate

There was an old lady who I thought was really nice.
My favourite meal at her house was curry and rice.
She had a dog,
She called him Mog,
For a reason I don't know.
Maybe it was 'cause she had no brains
From doing karate one hundred years ago!

Caitlin Hicks (9)
St John's CE Primary School, Worksop

The Storm

The sea was calm, it was quiet,
But then it turned into a riot,
The waves grew and grew
It was an amazing view,
The sky was covered with a black sheet,
The people huddle together for heat.

Aaron Emmerson (11)
St John's CE Primary School, Worksop

The Snail

The snail glides like a fish in the sea,
He pushes through the heavy grass
And leaves a silvery trail behind.
Antlers as gooey as tarmac
Pointing to the silvery, glowing moon.
What the courageous snail goes through to get his lunch.
The shell has the finest detail, no shell is identical.

Matthew Cook (8)
St Peter's CE (A) Primary School, Whetstone

Nature Springing Into Spring

The bees are busy buzzing
Making honey for their queen
The ants are making ant hills
Overnight, (they're very keen)

Some daffodils are growing
In the colour of bright yellow
The beetles crawl all over them
As if to say, 'Oh, hello!'

The squirrels eat the blossom
From the pinkish blossom trees
They do it oh so swiftly so that
No one ever sees

Ladybirds land on you
So you chant the special rhyme
Caterpillars into butterflies
Over periods of time

Bluebirds and other species
Make their twig and grass nests
They also lay their eggs so that
They can have a rest.

Emma Crossley (10)
St Peter's CE (A) Primary School, Whetstone

The Troublesome Trojan War

The wooden horse won it for them.

Like a baby's rattle, the Trojans so dumb,
They thought it was a present.
But did you know
this all started with the love of a Trojan?

Joel Plant (8)
St Peter's CE (A) Primary School, Whetstone

The Butterfly Lion

L ove in the air
I n England and Africa
O n a journey
N ever-ending love.

Danielle Cullen (9)
St Peter's CE (A) Primary School, Whetstone

Animal Life

Wake up in the morning,
Ponies, ponies gallop through the fields,
While bees are busy making honey
For all of us to eat.
Pigs are getting mucky, all covered in mud
And mothers of eggs are making a fuss.
What a busy year it's going to be.
Lots going on for us to see.
In the morning cars set off for work,
People at bus stops and children at school.
Wow, oh my, this is a busy year.
Seasons go round,
Winter, spring, summer and autumn,
All have new life for us to see.

Ellie Clarke (8)
Stickney CE Primary School, Boston

A Day In May

Day is beginning
Birds singing
Chickens clucking
People looking
Dogs running
Bees humming
Sun is shining
Picnic dining
Tall grass swaying
Children playing
People calling
Blossom falling
Sun is setting
Time for resting.

Mary Kate Cockburn (8)
Stickney CE Primary School, Boston

The Amazing Rainforest

While the trees grow,
The rivers flow
And the winds blow.

The trees sway,
This way and that way,
What a wondrous day!

A bird sings,
As it flaps its wings
In my ear it rings.

The rainforest is amazing,
It got me gazing,
As the hippos were grazing.

Jane Tega Akinola (11)
Thorplands Primary School, Northampton

Visit The Amazon

One, two, three, everybody come follow me.
You need to hear about the Amazon.
When you get there you just want to chill and relax.
If you get disturbed you will just be like Mad Max!
The grass is as green as a soldier's suit.
The huts are big and small, they are all made from straw.

When you walk you can see the blue, sparkling water for a mile.
All you can see are the boats in the water, they are big and small.
They can go up and down, side to side,
Like when you are on a roller coaster ride.
When you walk so far you have a pain in your feet
So you just want to take a seat.
Listen to the beat.

You can see monkeys in the trees sing and dance in the vines.
Hurry up and make up your minds
Because there is a snake that slides,
Birds that glide and gorillas that are big and wide.
The lizards are small and fast,
It's like they're having a blast!

When you hunt you'd better wear a mask,
It will be alright if you follow the task.
If you see an animal and you get scared,
You'd better call for your mum because I won't be there.
If you catch a disease you will call the doctor and be saying, 'Please.'
There are lots of flowers, if you look inside the flower
you can see bowers.
They are as small as grass and they can't run as fast as a slug,
They both run like a bug.
All the animals are different, that's what makes them good.
That's why you want to visit the Amazon.

Michael Connors (10)
Thorplands Primary School, Northampton

The Secrets Of The Rainforest

While I am in the jungle's trees
I feel a warm breeze
It is on the top of my knees
It feels like it's forty degrees
I also see monkeys
Picking and eating each other's fleas

The river flows as it grows
I find a log and start to row
All of a sudden I see a big, black crow
Did you know
The crow can grow
To a quarter of a metre or so?

The trees sway
The snakes lay
As the tiger cubs play
I say
Hip hip hooray!

So . . . the warm breeze and the monkeys
The river flows and the big, black crow
The trees sway as the tiger cubs play
I might come back another day.

Joshua Wise (11)
Thorplands Primary School, Northampton

Rainforest

The long grass sways side to side
The golden jaguar hunting for its food
The long grass helps hide the animals
Some trees seem a million years old
Snails trick animals; are they rocks?
Butterflies flutter from sticky, sparkling spider webs.

Alicia Cousins (9)
Thorplands Primary School, Northampton

The Rainforest In The Future

In the rainforest
It's good in the morning
Bad at night
In the evening it's calm.

The bananas taste like Heaven
The coconuts taste like Hell
The raspberries go wild.

The trees are bigger than skyscrapers
The leaves are bigger than snakes
The flowers the same size as ants.

Stick insects the same size as my little finger
Snakes the same size as me
Crocodiles bigger than me.

The flowers look like rainbows
The leaves look like grass
The mud looks like monkeys.

The heat could melt the North Pole
Hardly any coldness
It's just the right heat for me.

Ian Snelson (10)
Thorplands Primary School, Northampton

Untitled

Sweet-tasting berries, the fruit of the bush
Smooth, glowing, fresh fruit
Root relaxing tiredly underground
Silver, silky web leaning over an African land snail
The flower's fragrance drifting into noses of birds
Creepers follow the wind
The bugs follow the noise through the cave.

Esther Oluwatoyin Peter (9)
Thorplands Primary School, Northampton

The Rainforest

In the forest there are animals
Can you see them?
The monkeys are swinging and singing
The rainforest is as big as a giant
The trees are as tall as the Eiffel Tower
You can see the river shining like diamonds
When it rains it is as warm as the sun
When you look at the stars it is damp and pointy like a lion's claw
I can see the toucans squawking in the trees
And the butterflies fluttering
I can feel the warm, dark and damp bark
And the snails slithering across the ground
All I have to eat is bark and bugs
In the future I hope the animals and trees will be there
If they aren't, how can people be so cruel?
Why is it allowed?
Why is it only buildings?
Use the sea like a swimming pool.
Where are the animals going to go?
Is the world a horrid place or isn't it?
If it is, why do this?

Amy-Jo Jarvis (10)
Thorplands Primary School, Northampton

Rainforest

In the rainforest I heard a snake hissing,
Lots of animals are now missing.
In the rainforest I heard water trickling down the waterfall,
I saw a frog, it was a poisonous one, a big, blue one.
In the rainforest it was very hot on the ground, it was very muddy.
What a wonderful sight to see.

Eliza Brence (8)
Thorplands Primary School, Northampton

What's That Scent In The Rainforest?

The pink rose is as pink as can be
It is as pink as a pig
You can smell it for miles around
It smells as sweet as a cherry.

The golden flowers are as gold as a pound
They smell like some sweet honey
The children all want to eat it.

The red flowers smell like a tomato
They are as red as a strawberry
They light up the whole rainforest.

The white flower is as white as snow
You can smell it from miles away
It smells like an apple.

If there were no flowers
The world would be dull
Instead of smelling beautiful
It would smell like petrol.

That's the scent of the rainforest.

Emma Cormack (10)
Thorplands Primary School, Northampton

Rainforest Riddle

I am an animal that lives in the rainforest canopy.
I eat lots of fruits, insects, seeds and small animals.
I have a white face, with black all over my body.
I can live to be thirty-five or forty five years old.
If I lose my mother, another mother will bring me back to her.
I help trees grow all over the rainforest,
Because I eat fruit on one side and spit on the other side.
I am the white-faced capuchin monkey.

Imran Miah Khan (9)
Thorplands Primary School, Northampton

The Frog Led The Way

The mud squelched into my shoes
Creatures started to appear
Unusual I felt,
Unusual it was.

Carry on
Can't stop now, I thought
I moved on, into the forest.
Strange was in my mind
As a tree frog hopped onto my shoulder,
As if it were a decent gentleman.

Still on my shoulder,
The lightweight creature croaked
But then it bounced off, away
But I followed and was led to a tree
Inside there was a canopy
The frog had another friend
But that was a different story.

Jordan Buckle (11)
Thorplands Primary School, Northampton

Things In The Rainforest

Rough trees sway
Agile monkeys swing
Insects' songs vibrate and hum
Never still, always moving
Fruit, juicy and plump
Odours, both bitter and sweet
Raindrops sparkle like diamonds
Eager butterflies and flies
Snakes slither and slide
Tarantulas on the prowl.

Bolaji Orefuja (11)
Thorplands Primary School, Northampton

Rainforest Dream

In the Amazon the sounds you hear are relaxing,
The mud is like melted chocolate.
The waterfalls sparkle like diamonds
And the rain trickles down your face.
As you walk through the rainforest
You start to get really sweaty and clammy.

The fruit you see, if you try it, it's delicious
And there are lots of animals.
The jaguars are roaring, the monkeys are howling in the trees,
Swinging vine to vine.
The snakes slither through the grass.

When I touch the plants they are really smooth
and the tree trunks are rough.
I can smell the lovely flowers
But the sight you see will not be,
The rainforest will die.

Brandon Baxter (10)
Thorplands Primary School, Northampton

Rainforest

I saw a snake slither up my boot
And it tickled my foot.
It was so big
I ran away to have a fig.
Oh, what a sight to see.
Though it ran away from my tree
It looked like a she.
As raindrops dropped on my head
I felt like I was going to drop down dead.
I saw a monkey on my roof
So I told my mum to give it a book.

Oluwatomisin Orefuja (7)
Thorplands Primary School, Northampton

What Am I?

I look like a squiggly line in 3D,
I feel smooth and sometimes rough,
You can sometimes find me scaly,
I dream of having peace in the world,
As I slither across the floor I sway side to side,
The tree stumps make my body bump.
I very rarely eat eggs,
But when I do they are sometimes hard and rough.
I dream I have a longer body,
I dream to be kept nicely
So people can sponsor me,
Because we are getting rare.
I sometimes camouflage myself
To stay hidden from danger,
I can hear monkeys chattering,
Trees swaying and sticks snapping.

Daryl Keightley (11)
Thorplands Primary School, Northampton

The Amazon Rainforest

The rainforest is really sunny,
Sometime it can get a little loud when you go there,
You will love it,
It's like a magical place to be.

In the rainforest you can smell fresh fruits and tropical flowers
And you can taste fresh fruits and you can hear animals playing
And the waterfall pouring and you can also touch the trees.

The sky is as blue as bluebells
And the mud is as deep as the deep end of the swimming pool.
The rainforest has a lot of things in it
Like flowers, trees and waterfalls.

Zainab Adebisi (10)
Thorplands Primary School, Northampton

Magical Rainforest

As I walk through the rainforest calmly
Sweet, juicy fruits I see.
Colourful parrots fly in the sky,
Travelling amazingly high.
Agile monkeys swing from tree to tree,
In the perfumed, aromatic breeze.
Next to the shiny, blue river
A lot of snakes like to slither.
On lily pads frogs leap,
As it becomes dark they begin to sleep.
Day becomes night,
Sun becomes moon,
Tiny birds sing a peaceful tune.

Abigail Harvey (10)
Thorplands Primary School, Northampton

Rainforest In The Modern World

In the rainforest I can feel raindrops rolling down my cheek
In the modern world I can feel the heat
In the rainforest I can hear the birds go *tweet, tweet*
In the modern world I can hear children playing in the sea.

In the rainforest I can hear lions roar
In the modern world I can eat more and more
In the rainforest the birds are as colourful as exotic fruit
In the modern world I can smell tropical fruit.

In the rainforest I can touch a snake
In the modern world I can buy a cake
In the rainforest I see a frog
In the modern world I walk my dog.

Jazz Bilalaj (10)
Thorplands Primary School, Northampton

The Mysterious World

The rainforest trees swaying,
The monkeys playing,
The waters flow,
As the plants grow,
I begin to sense,
That it is dense.

As I hear the parrots squawking,
I start gawking,
Then I start gazing
As the hippos are grazing.
Exotic animals bounce,
As the birds flounce.

Mojibola Orefuja (11)
Thorplands Primary School, Northampton

The Rainforest

In the rainforest there is a beautiful bunch of flowers
That smell beautiful
The golden sun blazes down on the flowers

The floor of the rainforest looks like chocolate melting
Sounds delicious! Yum-yum!
Look at the tree, it is bumpy, like a rock
Its leaves are all different shades of green

Wow, look at the river
The rock looks like sparkling diamonds
The fish are as big as whales
Their colours look like rainbows.

Joshua Richards (10)
Thorplands Primary School, Northampton

Save The Rainforest

R ainforests
A re beautiful and full of animals
I n danger, from poachers and tree choppers
N early dying out, leaving animals homeless
F orever will it be here?
O K, let's save the rainforest!
R ainforest must stay!
E nvironmental responsibility is ours!
S o let's save the rainforest.
T ogether we can!

Hayley Locke (10)
Thorplands Primary School, Northampton

Rainforest

In the rainforest I saw a snake slithering
Then a jaguar started running
Then I heard a waterfall
Then I heard a squawk from a bird in the bush.
Then I saw a blue, poisonous frog.
In the rainforest it is hot
And it is mostly raining.
The sun comes out when it is raining in the rainforest
And the rainbow follows
In the rainforest.

Jodene White (8)
Thorplands Primary School, Northampton

Anger

I was angry, I felt sad
Because I had to go to the head teacher's office
I was late for school.
Uh oh, I had an itch!
Ouch, ouch, ouch!
Scratch, scratch, scratch
I asked my friend to help me
So she did
Then I felt happier.

Chloe Finch (8)
Thorplands Primary School, Northampton

The Rainforest

As I walk into the rainforest
I taste the fresh, aromatic air of the rainforest.
I see lots of strange creatures coming for me.
I feel a tingly feeling on my legs,
I look down,
I am terrified by what I see,
It is lots of leeches sucking at my leg.
I shake them off.
I can hear frogs croaking now.

William Tague (11)
Thorplands Primary School, Northampton

Rainforest

Slimy, rushing, oozing water with aromatic fruit,
Hanging there, about to fall off the emerald tree.
The wind flows through the tree, making the fruit fall
Onto the ground.

Matthew Tague (9)
Thorplands Primary School, Northampton

Rainforest

Knotted roots lurking over plants.
Fruit hanging from emerald leaves.
Spider's, silver, silky, smooth web.
Beautiful blooming heliotrope flower.
Grass twisted between vines.
Smooth, aromatic, fresh fruit.
Waterfalls as diamond as can be.
Colours flashing by plants;
Gold petals on the flower.

Reece Haynes (9)
Thorplands Primary School, Northampton

The Monkeys, So Lovely

The trees were swaying in front of my face
As I walked through the misty forest.
All of a sudden creatures started to appear,
They stared at me, but I had to carry on.
Then I saw a monkey, it started to lead me somewhere.
It led me to its home, it smelt like perfume,
All the monkeys were lovely,
But I couldn't stay there, it was getting dark.

Anthony Lyttle (11)
Thorplands Primary School, Northampton

My Rainforest Poem

It's hot and steamy and the sun is gleaming
Whilst birds sing and dance in the heat
The monkeys scream from tree to tree
The frogs jump near the flowing water
And the butterflies shimmer in the heat.

Sophie McKay (10)
Thorplands Primary School, Northampton

Rainforest

I heard a lion roar,
A frog jumped on its paw.
The lion scratched me with his claws
And then it had a fright and then kicked a pipe.
It turned on a tap and then it had a slap around the face.
It kicked Wally and he met Polly,
The lion lay on the mat and the cat scratched his hat
And then he killed the cat on the mat.

Connor King (7)
Thorplands Primary School, Northampton

The Rainforest Rhythm

Cassowary creeping quickly
Spider scattering on his sticky, gleaming web
Plump, juicy fruit hanging happily
Ready to be eaten
Snakes slithering in snail slime
Parrots squawking squeakily
Sun shining like gold
Flowers like diamonds.

Taylor-Mae Miller (9)
Thorplands Primary School, Northampton

The Rainforest Poem

Sticky branches
Plump fruit hangs from the tree
In a cheeky way
Birds tweeting high up in the trees
Crispy, hard mud on the floor.

Elizabeth McLean (9)
Thorplands Primary School, Northampton

Untitled

Snake slithered through the slippery, green grass,
Lots of fruit on the trees
Pineapples, oranges and bananas,
Birds as fast as a plane.

Bethany Byram (8)
Thorplands Primary School, Northampton

Young Writers Information

We hope you have enjoyed reading this book - and that you will continue to enjoy it in the coming years.

If you like reading and writing poetry drop us a line, or give us a call, and we'll send you a free information pack.

Alternatively if you would like to order further copies of this book or any of our other titles, then please give us a call or log onto our website at www.youngwriters.co.uk.

A platform for your poetry!

Young Writers Information
Remus House
Coltsfoot Drive
Peterborough
PE2 9JX
(01733) 890066

Get in touch!